SHARE JESUS

LIKE IT MATTERS

STEVE GAINES

Auxano
PRESS

Dedication

I dedicate this book to a sweet woman I have never met.

In 1951, when my mother was only twenty-four years old, she was diagnosed with cancer in both breasts. One breast was removed, and the other was to be removed the next day. My mother's roommate at the hospital, who already had a double mastectomy herself, climbed up in my mother's bed and prayed all night for God to heal her. Indeed, God miraculously healed her that night. The doctors discovered her cancer was gone! When my mother came out from under anesthesia, her roommate shared Jesus with her and led my mother to faith in Him. Mother returned to Central City, Kentucky and was baptized in a Baptist church. My father was saved shortly after. That is why I grew up in a Baptist church, heard the Gospel, and was saved. I look forward to meeting that sweet woman in Heaven one day who prayed in faith for my mother's healing, and then shared Jesus with her like it mattered. Indeed, it mattered to my mom and dad, and it still matters to me!

Foreword

Bill Sullivan wasn't someone you heard preach at a conference. He never wrote a book. He wasn't even a pastor. He was a layperson from a Southern Baptist church who believed the gospel had the power to change lives.

One night many years ago Bill had a conversation about Jesus with a young, twenty-something couple named Mike and Glenda. They came to faith in Christ that night. A few days later I stood on a pew and watched my parents get baptized. I never met Bill Sullivan and I didn't fully understand what my parents did that night, but that gospel conversation changed my parents' lives for eternity.

And it changed the trajectory of their three children, 13 grandchildren and one great-grandchild too.

I'm forever grateful that this Baptist layman took the time to share Jesus with my parents that night.

I'm convinced that for the church in North America to make a dent in our continent's lostness, we need more Bill Sullivans. The North American church needs more believers actively engaging their neighbors and coworkers in gospel conversations.

That's why I am excited about this book Steve has put together. He is calling churches and individual Christians back to our core purpose—to know God and to bring Him glory by introducing more people to Him.

A major threat to the evangelical church in North America today is that so many have plateaued or are declining in membership. In the faith group I serve—Southern Baptists—we lose an average of 1,000 churches every year. Most of them have simply locked their doors and died. It is such a crisis that at the North American Mission Board where I lead, we have made church revitalization and church re-planting a major priority. It is not a problem unique to Southern Baptists.

Why are so many churches dying? We have found that by far the most common reason is that at some point the congregation turned inward. They started focusing mostly on ministries that served themselves. Good things probably, but they lost their focus on the outside world around them. Individuals stopped sharing their faith with non-believers. The church stopped connecting with its community. The salt lost its taste. The light grew dim.

That's why *Share Jesus Like It Matters* is such an important book. Of course mostly because it really does matter to those with whom we are sharing. When Bill Sullivan shared Jesus with my father, it dramatically changed the course of his life, my mom's life and our entire family. Probably just within your church there are families that can share similar stories. One life changed can lead to so many others.

But sharing Jesus also matters for other reasons. When we follow Jesus' command to make disciples we are being obedient to Him. When we don't we are disobedient. There are blessings that come from obedience and consequences for disobedience. Watch what happens when you start to obediently share your faith. You will be amazed how many people God will put in your path and you will be encouraged beyond measure as you have the privilege of watching lives change before your eyes.

And what will happen to our churches? Instead of the stagnation and death that comes from an inward focus, our churches will come alive. When more Christians start having gospel conversations that will lead to gospel congregations. The light will shine. The salt regains its flavor.

For years many Southern Baptist churches faithfully used the Home Mission Board's Continuing Witness Training (CWT) material to equip believers to share their faith. It was a great tool that helped thousands of believers take the gospel to friends and neighbors. Now we have given that resource to Steve to use in conjunction with this book. I can't wait to see how his passion and enthusiasm for the gospel will bring new life to this great resource.

If you are a pastor, I hope you will embrace this book and discover how it can help transform your congregation from an inward focus to an outward mission. If you are an individual believer, I challenge you to put into practice the approaches shared here. You will see how quickly God starts to use you and you will be amazed at the encouragement and spiritual growth it will bring.

Dr. Kevin Ezell
President
North American Mission Board, SBC
Alpharetta, Georgia

Contents

Introduction

June 14, 1980 will always be a special day for me. It was the day I married Donna Dodds. Donna and I met in college, dated for a year and a half, and then we married. Frankly, I would have married her after our first date! She loved the Lord, she was beautiful, and she felt called to serve in full-time Christian ministry. After we prayed on that first date, I knew it was the beginning of something that would last for a lifetime.

After our wedding ceremony, we drove to the hotel. En route, we both became thirsty and stopped at a Dairy Queen to buy soft drinks. I walked into that tiny fast-food restaurant in Jackson, Tennessee, and something came over me. Before I knew it, I shouted out to everyone present, "I just got married!" The place immediately erupted with cheers and applause. We celebrated together, I purchased our soft drinks, and then went back to the car and told Donna what I had done. We laughed and drove away. I had shared some really good news that I just could not keep to myself!

Have you ever been so excited about something that you had to share it with others? That's the way it should be with every Christian. We should be so enthusiastic about the fact that Jesus is our Lord and Savior that we cannot contain the good news.

I remember the first person I ever led to Christ. He was a cafeteria worker at a Fellowship of Christian Athletes' camp in North Carolina. I was an eighteen-year-old college student, alone with this stranger, doing the best I could to share Jesus with him. Then came that moment when I asked if he would like to follow Jesus. My heart was beating rapidly when he answered, "Yes, I would." I then helped him call on the name of the Lord for salvation by leading him in a "sinner's prayer" through which he *repented* of his sin, *believed* that Jesus died for his sins and rose from the dead, and *received* Jesus as his Lord and Savior. Afterwards, I gave him a Bible and encouraged him to read a chapter a day in the Gospel of John. We prayed together, shook hands, and parted ways.

I was on cloud nine! I'll never forget what it felt like to lead someone to faith in Jesus. It changed his life and mine. Nothing is more thrilling and fulfilling for a Christian than to lead a lost person to Jesus. That night, I asked the Lord to help me become a soul-winner.

Admittedly, since then, I've been slack at times in my efforts to share Jesus. Yet the Lord has helped me to discipline myself to witness and share the Gospel one-on-one with many lost people.

As a senior pastor since 1983, I have seen many people give their hearts to Christ after I have preached Gospel sermons in public settings. Yet I can honestly say that I still get more excited when God uses me to lead one lost person to Him through personal evangelism than I do when people get saved after I preach. Again, nothing is as thrilling as leading someone to faith in Jesus Christ. Absolutely nothing!

We live in a day when personal evangelism is in a state of decline among evangelical Christians, even among my own faith family, the Southern Baptist Convention. At the time of this writing, our seminary enrollments may be up a little. However, our baptismal numbers for new converts are down—way down. Many leaders in our day emphasize "making disciples," and rightfully so (cf. Matt. 28:18-20). But too often, "making disciples" has degenerated into simply gathering together people who are already Christians to engage in Bible study, prayer, Scripture memory, and so forth. They might occasionally go on a mission trip or enjoy fellowship at someone's home. But rarely, if ever, do they verbally share the Gospel with lost people.

Is that what Jesus had in mind when He commanded His followers in the first century to "make disciples of all the nations"? Absolutely not! To *make* a disciple obviously includes first sharing Jesus and winning a lost person to faith in Christ.

Jesus commands His followers in Matthew 28:18-20 to (1) make disciples, (2) baptize disciples, and (3) teach disciples. Again, the phrase, *make disciples* includes sharing Jesus with lost people. It involves leading them from a state of being lost and en route to Hell to a state of being born again, regenerated by the Spirit of God, and on their way to Heaven. If not, then there is no evangelism in the text above that we refer to as the *Great Commission*. The earliest Christians were evangelistic soul-winners that verbally shared Jesus with lost people!

At Bellevue Baptist Church, our mission statement is: "Love God, Love People, Share Jesus, and Make Disciples."

That third part of our Mission Statement—*Share Jesus*—is crucial. At Bellevue, we have four questions that we ask ourselves constantly to measure whether we are accomplishing our mission to "Share Jesus." Those questions are:

- Am I prepared to share the Gospel?
- Am I proactively developing relationships with lost people?
- Am I engaged in local witnessing opportunities?
- Am I taking the Gospel to the nations?

These four measures help us focus on engaging in biblical, intentional, verbal evangelism. Because of these measures, we are more likely to share Jesus with lost people and win them to Him in salvation.

I wrote a book on prayer entitled *Pray Like It Matters*.[1] The title came from my conviction that when we pray, God does things that He would not have done had we not prayed. Our prayers really do matter in what happens on earth. When we touch God in Heaven with our prayers, God touches earth with His answers. Our lives are literally the culmination and result of both the prayers we have prayed and the prayers we have not prayed. Undeniably, our prayers matter. Prayer "changes things."

In the same regard, when we share the Gospel with lost people, God saves people that He would not have saved had we not shared Jesus. Our sharing Jesus/witnessing/evange-

---

[1] Steve Gaines, *Pray Like It Matters*, (Tigerville, South Carolina, Auxano Press, 2013).

lism/soul-winning *does* matter! When we share Jesus, people will enjoy a higher quality of life during their time on earth than they would have apart from Christ. They will also go to Heaven when they die instead of going to Hell.

As I mentioned earlier, sharing Jesus/witnessing/evangelism/soul-winning has fallen on hard times. The very term, *soul-winning*, is often labeled as archaic or antiquated among modern evangelical Christians.

Nevertheless, soul-winning *is* a biblical concept! The Apostle Paul said,

> *What then is my reward? That, when I preach the gospel, I may offer the gospel without charge, so as not to make full use of my right in the gospel. For though I am free from all men, I have made myself a slave to all, so that I may win more. To the Jews I became as a Jew, so that I might win Jews; to those who are under the Law, as under the Law though not being myself under the Law, so that I might win those who are under the Law; to those who are without law, as without law, though not being without the law of God but under the law of Christ, so that I might win those who are without law. To the weak I became weak, that I might win the weak; I have become all things to all men, so that I may by all means save some. I do all things for the sake of the gospel, so that I may become a fellow partaker of it. Do you not know that those who run in a race all run, but only one receives the prize? Run in such a way that you may win (1 Cor. 9:18-24).*

Paul uses the word *win* six times in this text to refer to leading people to faith in Jesus. Paul was a soul-*win*ner! Likewise, God wants you to run the Christian race "in such a way that you may win" lost people to Jesus!

I have written *Share Jesus Like It Matters* for two reasons. First, I want to show you *why* you should share Jesus with lost people. Second, I want to show you *how* you can share Jesus with lost people. In the following pages you will learn how to identify, pray for, and share Jesus with non-Christians.

I encourage you to commit to memory the Scripture verses listed in these chapters as well as the Gospel outline. You will learn how to intentionally, proactively, scripturally, politely, and verbally engage people with the Gospel. When that happens, you *will* see results. Some will reject Jesus; others will accept Him. Regardless, your job is to give them the Gospel. Your witnessing will honor Christ, bless you, and change the lives and eternities of those with whom you share!

Christian, it's time for you to win precious souls to Christ. It's time for you to *Share Jesus Like It Matters*!

Steve Gaines, PhD
Senior Pastor
Bellevue Baptist Church
Memphis, TN

Chapter 1
What It Means to Share Jesus

"Then Philip opened his mouth, and
beginning from this Scripture he
preached Jesus to him." (Acts 8:35)

One of the most effective evangelistic Christians in the early
church was a man named Philip. He was one of the seven
original deacons in the church at Jerusalem (cf. Acts 6). When
persecution came from the Jewish leaders against the early
Christians, many believers left Jerusalem. As they traveled
away from Jerusalem, they went to other areas in Judea and
also in Samaria. As they went, they shared Jesus. The Bible
says in Acts 8:4, "Therefore, those who had been scattered
went about preaching the word."

Philip went to Samaria and shared Jesus with them (Acts
8:5f). God also performed many miracles through him which
caused the crowds to gather and listen intently to his Gospel
message. As Philip ministered, people were saved, healed,
and set free from demonic strongholds. Great joy came to
that area. Many in Samaria were saved by repenting of their
sin and believing in Jesus. Philip baptized them. When the
leaders in the church at Jerusalem heard what God was
doing through Philip in Samaria, they sent the Apostles Peter
and John to assist.

The revival taking place in Samaria was a fulfillment of Jesus' parting words in Acts 1:8. Our Lord had commissioned His disciples to begin their witnessing in Jerusalem, and then to branch out into the regions of Judea and Samaria. God allowed the persecution of His people to move them out of Jerusalem and into the broader spiritual harvest fields around them, including Samaria where Philip was ministering.

In the midst of that great movement of God in Samaria, the Lord directed Philip to leave and go to an isolated area to share Jesus with one man. An angel commanded Philip to go south to a road that led out of Jerusalem toward the desert area of Gaza (Acts 8:26). The man with whom Philip was to share was a prominent man from Ethiopia. He was "an Ethiopian eunuch, a court official of Candace, queen of the Ethiopians, who was in charge of all her treasure; and he had come to Jerusalem to worship" (Acts 8:27).

As the eunuch rode in his chariot on that desert road, He was reading a messianic text from the Old Testament book of Isaiah. The Holy Spirit commanded Philip to join him. Philip heard the eunuch reading Scripture and asked him if he understood what he was reading. The man indicated that he could use some help in understanding the meaning of Isaiah's text. That's when Philip went up into the man's chariot and shared Jesus with Him.

Acts 8:35 is one of the greatest verses in the New Testament when it comes to describing the essence of evangelism (sharing Jesus). Philip did three things: (1) he opened his mouth and spoke, (2) he based all he said on the authority of Scripture, and (3) he focused the conversation on Jesus Christ. *That* is evangelism—*verbally sharing what the Bible says about Jesus.* That is what we are emphasizing with the title *"Share Jesus Like It Matters."*

Philip went on to lead the man to faith in Christ and baptize him. The eunuch's baptism is also a beautiful picture of what biblical baptism is: (1) for believers only, (2) by immersion only, and (3) a symbol of one's salvation.

In this chapter we will look first at what it does not mean to share Jesus. We will then look at what it does mean to share Jesus. We will analyze the meaning of the New Testament word *euangelion* and then conclude by looking at a classic definition of evangelism.

What "Sharing Jesus" Is *Not*

Some Christians believe that basically all activities of the church are evangelism. They justify this idea by stressing that at least in some abstract way, evangelism is at the heart of everything the church does. That would be wonderful if true, but unfortunately it isn't. The fact is, many churches are involved in multiple activities that are not equivalent with sharing the Gospel intentionally with a lost person. A better umbrella term for "everything the church does" might be ministry, but it certainly shouldn't be evangelism.

For instance, working in the nursery is ministry, but it is not sharing Jesus. Likewise, parking cars for senior adults is ministry, but it is not sharing Jesus. Greeting people at the church door and welcoming them is a valuable ministry, but technically it is not sharing Jesus. Even though caring for children, assisting senior adults, and welcoming people to the church campus all assist the preacher as he shares the Gospel of Jesus in the worship service, these are not intrinsically forms of "sharing Jesus." All ministry is not sharing Jesus.

Churches of a more liberal theological persuasion often view social ministry—meeting a hurting person's physical needs—as a form of sharing Jesus. I have talked with theologically liberal pastors who contend that when they reach out in compassion and love to meet the physical needs of others, they are in their own way "leading" those people to the Savior.

Christians are indeed commanded to meet the needs of our fellow human beings who are suffering and hurting, but if all we do is meet their physical needs without seeking to meet their more important, spiritual need for salvation, then we only make their situation in life a better place from which to go to Hell. Social ministry and meeting the physical needs of others can provide an excellent platform for sharing Jesus, but by itself, it is not New Testament evangelism.

I have also known of liberal churches and Christians that teach that all people will eventually go to Heaven. Theologically, such people are called Universalists. They believe God's salvation is universal in that God will "universally" grant salvation to all people. They assert that God is love (1 John 4:7-8), and being a loving God, He would never send anyone to Hell. But the same Bible that says God is love also says He is holy (1 Pet. 1:15). He is righteous (2 Tim. 4:8), and He must punish sin

(Nah. 1:3; Rom. 6:23). God is even referred to in Scripture as a God of wrath (Rom. 1:18; Eph. 5:6).

Jesus Himself spoke frequently about the reality of both Heaven and Hell. He spoke not only of a Heaven to gain but also of a Hell to shun (Matt. 25:46). According to Scripture, all people are *not* going to Heaven. Jesus actually taught that most people will go to Hell (Matt. 7:13-14). In fact, Jesus said that many who think they are saved and on their way to Heaven will actually be informed by God at the final judgment that they are lost and on their way to Hell (Matt. 7:21f).

Jesus taught that people go to either Heaven or Hell based on what they do with Him during this short life on earth. Thus, sharing Jesus is not telling everyone that they are already saved, regardless of his or her relationship with Jesus. Telling them that would be a lie. And a lie is not "good news."

What *Is* "Sharing Jesus"?

So what does it mean to share Jesus? First, we will look at the Greek word *euangelion* that means, "good news." Second, we will consider an excellent definition of evangelism (i.e., sharing Jesus) by Dr. Roy Fish.

Sharing Jesus and Euangelion

"Evangelism" is an English transliteration of the Greek word euangelion. Throughout the New Testament it refers to the "good news" of the saving message concerning Jesus Christ.

In one of His first sermons, Jesus spoke these words in Mark 1:15, "The time is fulfilled, and the kingdom of God is at hand; repent and believe in the gospel [euangelion]." That good news changed lives and enabled people to turn from their sin and turn in faith to God.

Jesus also taught that the Gospel is worthy of one's complete devotion. He said in Mark 8:35, "For whoever wishes to save his life will lose it, but whoever loses his life for My sake and the gospel's [euangelion] will save it."

Likewise, the Apostle Paul spoke frequently about sharing the Gospel. Indeed, Paul would share Jesus with anyone at any time, refusing to be ashamed of the Gospel. He said in Romans 1:16, "For I am not ashamed of the *gospel* [euangelion], for it is the power of God for salvation to everyone who believes, to the Jew first and also to the Greek."

Paul also stressed that everything he did was for the purpose of verbally sharing Jesus with lost people. He said in 1 Corinthians 9:23, "I do all things for the sake of the *gospel* [euangelion], so that I may become a fellow partaker of it."

Thus, the word "Gospel" (euangelion) refers to the "Good News" about Jesus Christ's sacrificial death and victorious resurrection that brings salvation to a lost sinner when he repents and believes in Jesus.

A Definition of Evangelism (Sharing Jesus)

In the 1980s, I attended Southwestern Baptist Theological Seminary in Fort Worth, Texas. One of the most popular professors at Southwestern was Dr. Roy Fish, professor of evangelism. Here is his insightful definition of "evangelism" (i.e., sharing Jesus):

> *Evangelism is the compassionate sharing of the Good News of Jesus Christ in the power of the Holy Spirit to lost people with the intent of winning them to Christ as Lord and Savior that they in turn might share Him with others.*

In his definition, Dr. Fish speaks of:

The *Spirit* of Evangelism— compassionate. Like Jesus, Christians must love lost people. When Jesus looked at lost multitudes, He felt compassion for them (Matt. 9:35-38). He also felt a genuine love for individuals with whom he shared the Gospel (Mark 10:17-22).

The *Communication* of Evangelism— sharing. If you want to share Jesus, you must set a good example for lost people, but you must also *verbally* share the Gospel of Jesus as Philip did with the Ethiopian eunuch (Acts 8:35).

The *Content* of Evangelism— the good news of Jesus Christ. The Gospel focuses on Jesus' atoning death for sinners, His burial to verify His death, and His bodily resurrection from the dead (1 Cor. 15:3-4). Any message short of this is *not* sharing Jesus!

The *Power* of Evangelism— the Holy Spirit. Christians rely on the power of the Holy Spirit to embolden them to share Jesus (Acts 1:8). We also rely on the Spirit to convict lost people of their sinfulness, their lack of righteousness, and the judgment of God to come (John 16:8). The Holy Spirit also converts the repentant, believing sinner by transacting regeneration, the new birth (John 3:5-9; Titus 3:5).

The *Recipients* of Evangelism— lost people. People who do not know Jesus as Lord and Savior are spiritually *lost*. Jesus compared a lost sinner to a lost sheep, lost silver, and a lost son (Luke 15). Also, after Jesus saved Zacchaeus, our Lord confirmed that His mission on earth was to seek and to save people who were "lost" (Luke 19:10).

The *Purpose* of Evangelism— winning them to Christ as Lord and Savior. The Christian's goal in verbally sharing Jesus is to *win* lost people to Christ. The Apostle Paul sought to defer to people and serve them in various ways so he could *win* them to faith in Christ (1 Cor. 9:19-23). Paul also commanded all Christians to "run in such a way that [they] might *win*" lost people to Jesus (1 Cor. 9:24).

The *Perpetuation* of Evangelism— that they in turn might share Him with others. Mature Christian believers should urgently train all new Christians to share Jesus as soon as possible. One reason is because immediately after their conversion to Christ new disciples often have more connections with non-Christians than at any other time later on. Consider Matthew (Levi). Immediately after he became Christ's disciple, he contacted many of his lost friends and invited them, as well as Jesus and His disciples, to his home for dinner (Luke 5:27f). That illustrates why one important aspect of the Great Commission is to teach new believers to observe all that Christ commands us (Matt. 28:19-20), which unquestionably includes sharing Jesus.

Challenge:

When is the last time you *verbally* shared what the Bible says about Jesus with a lost person with the intention of leading that person to salvation in Him?

Read, reread, and perhaps memorize Dr. Fish's outstanding definition of evangelism. It will be a constant reminder to show you what it really means to share Jesus with the lost.

For Memory and Meditation:

"Then Philip opened his mouth, and beginning from this Scripture he preached Jesus to him" (Acts 8:35).

Chapter 2
Our Commission to Share Jesus

"Go therefore and make disciples of all
the nations" (Matt. 28:19).

"Go into all the world and preach the gospel to all creation"
(Mark 16:15).

"And that repentance for forgiveness of sins would be
proclaimed in His name to all the nations, beginning from
Jerusalem. You are witnesses of these things" (Luke 24:47-48).

"As the Father has sent Me, I also send you" (John 20:21).

"But you will receive power when the Holy Spirit has come
upon you; and you shall be My witnesses" (Acts 1:8).

Christ commissioned every Christian to verbally share the
Gospel with lost people for the purpose of winning them to
Himself. As we learned in the previous chapter, deacon Philip
witnessed to the Ethiopian eunuch in Acts 8:35 by verbally
sharing what the Bible says about Jesus. That is God's will
for each of His children. When it comes to sharing Jesus, no
believer in Christ is exempt.

Yet, in spite of Jesus' clear commissions, numerous
Christians live as though they are not responsible for shar-

ing Jesus with lost people. Many believe that sharing Jesus is the responsibility of others—perhaps the pastor, church staff members, deacons, or Sunday school teachers, but not themselves.

I have known Christians who have sought to dismiss Jesus' command to evangelize lost people by saying, "Evangelism is just not my spiritual gift." But the fact is, evangelism (sharing Jesus) is *never* referred to in the New Testament as a spiritual gift. While the New Testament does refer to the biblical *office* of "evangelist" (Eph. 4:11), it never refers to the spiritual *gift* of evangelism. The office of evangelist refers to specific men (evangelists) that God has called to serve in an evangelistic harvest ministry through their preaching and teaching. Again, Philip, a deacon, also served in the biblical office of evangelist (Acts 21:8). But that does *not* mean that Philip and other God-called evangelists were the only ones commissioned by God to share Jesus with lost people.

All Christians, including *all* pastors, are to evangelize by verbally sharing the Gospel. The Apostle Paul commanded his favorite son in the ministry, Timothy, who served as a *pastor*, to fulfill his ministry by "Do[ing] the work of an evangelist" (2 Tim. 4:5). Whenever Timothy preached the word of God, he was to share Jesus and call people to *repent* of their sins, *believe* in Jesus, and *receive* Him as Lord and Savior.

At least five times in the New Testament, Jesus commissioned, and thus commanded, *all* of His disciples to verbally share the Gospel with lost people. Let's look at those commissions now.

Jesus' Commission in the Gospel of Matthew

Jesus' first commission is found at the end of Matthew's Gospel. It is commonly referred to as the "Great Commission."

> And Jesus came up and spoke to them, saying, "All authority has been given to Me in Heaven and on earth. Go therefore and make disciples of all the nations, baptizing them in the name of the Father and the Son and the Holy Spirit, teaching them to observe all that I commanded you; and lo, I am with you always, even to the end of the age" (Matt. 28:18-20).

Jesus commanded His disciples to "make" new "disciples." Making disciples obviously includes sharing Jesus with lost people and winning them to Christ. Otherwise, there is no evangelism in the Great Commission. When God saves someone, He *makes* that person a new disciple. People do not become a Christian through salvation and then later become a disciple of Jesus. Instead, *every* Christian is a disciple of Jesus—either an obedient one or a disobedient one.

After a person becomes a disciple of Jesus through regeneration, Jesus commands that person to be baptized. Biblical baptism is exclusively by immersion (never sprinkling or pouring). It is done in the name (authority) of the triune God. Baptism has no saving power in and of itself. Rather, it is a symbolic picture, a sermon, of: (1) the death, burial and resurrection of Jesus, and (2) the believer's death to his former way of life, his spiritual burial into Christ, and his being raised to walk in newness of life. Again, baptism is symbolic, not salvific. Water cannot save anyone; only the blood of Jesus can!

Christian baptism is also exclusively for believers. The only people in the New Testament who were baptized were those who had already *repented* of their sins, *believed* in Jesus, and *received* Him as Lord and Savior. They were knowledgeable enough and thus accountable to willfully choose Christ as Savior. The New Testament never speaks of any baby being baptized. The words *baby* and *baptism* are not found together in the New Testament.

After baptism, according to Jesus' words in Matthew 28:18-20, all believers are to be taught Christ's commands, the first of which is to share Jesus and make disciples. An examination of Jesus' commission in Matthew's Gospel stresses at least three things:

Our *authority* for sharing Jesus and making disciples comes directly from Jesus Himself (v. 18). If someone asks us who gave us the right to say that salvation is only in Jesus, our answer is, "Jesus!" All our authority to share the Gospel comes from Him.

Our *assignment* for sharing Jesus is to *make* disciples, *baptize* disciples, and *teach* disciples" (vv. 19-20a). We are to win people to Christ, baptize them and connect them to a local church, and then help them begin growing in grace.

Our *assurance* for sharing Jesus is that as we focus on sharing Him and making disciples, baptizing disciples, and teaching disciples, then God promises that His manifest presence will empower us for His glory until the end of time (v. 20b).

This commission shows that all Christians are to verbally share what the Bible says about Jesus with lost people to win them to Him!

Jesus' Commission in the Gospel of Mark

Jesus' next commission is found at the end of Mark's Gospel. Though taken from a text not found in the earliest and most reliable Greek manuscripts of the New Testament, many Christians across the centuries have referred to it as a clear command from our Lord to witness to the lost.

> And He said to them, "Go into all the world and preach the gospel to all creation. He who has believed and has been baptized shall be saved; but he who has disbelieved shall be condemned" (Mark 16:15-16).

Again, Jesus gave comprehensive statements insisting that *all* believers are to share the Gospel with *everyone* throughout the entire world. Every Christian is under obligation to share Jesus because all lost people need to hear the Gospel message.

Jesus said whoever believes will be saved, and whoever does not believe will be condemned. Verse 16 adds, "He who has believed and has been baptized shall be saved." Unfor-

14

tunately, based on a misunderstanding of this text, some have erroneously sought to add baptism as a requirement for salvation. But in the same verse (v. 16), Jesus said that it is only those who have "disbelieved" who will be "condemned." In that verse, Jesus made no reference to baptism at all. If baptism had been God's requirement for salvation, it would have been included in both parts of verse 16. This single mention simply points out how important baptism is for the Christian's sanctification and spiritual growth in Christ. However, this text does not teach that baptism is a requirement for being saved.

Jesus' Commission in the Gospel of Luke

Some deny that Jesus commissioned His followers to evangelize in Luke's Gospel. Yet the disciples were clearly commissioned by our Lord to share Jesus in Luke 24:

> And He said to them, "Thus it is written, that the Christ would suffer and rise again from the dead the third day, and that repentance for forgiveness of sins would be proclaimed in His name to all the nations, beginning from Jerusalem. You are witnesses of these things" (vv. 46-48).

Before He ascended back to Heaven from the Mount of Olives, Jesus spoke these words to His disciples. He emphasized to them the essential truths of the Gospel—His vicarious death and His victorious resurrection. He then laid down the mandate that people must *repent* of their sins if they desire to have their sins forgiven in salvation. *Repent* means to do a spiritual "about-face," to make a spiritual "U-turn." Repentance is a change of mind and heart that results in a change of life and action, all wrought by the Holy Spirit. Repentance is still the message we are to emphasize when we share Jesus.

Jesus said, "I tell you, no, but unless you repent, you will all likewise perish" (Luke 13:3). Later, the Apostle Paul told a group of lost intellectuals at Athens that "God is now declaring to men that all people everywhere should *repent*" (Acts 17:30).

Jesus' commission in Luke's Gospel commands every Christian to tell lost people to repent of their sin, turn to God, and place their faith in Christ so they can freely and willfully receive Him as Lord and Savior.

Jesus' Commission in the Gospel of John

John's Gospel is perhaps the most evangelistic of all the four Gospels. Toward the end of this Gospel, Jesus commissioned His disciples to be His witnesses with the following words:

> So Jesus said to them again, "Peace be with you; as the Father has sent Me, I also send you."
> (John 20:21).

John stressed that Jesus was sent from God to make salvation available to all people. Arguably the most famous verse of scripture in the Bible, John 3:16, clearly states, "For

God so loved *the world*, that He gave His only begotten Son, that *whoever* believes in Him shall not perish, but have eternal life." Jesus affirmed in that text that God loves *everyone* in the world, and that *anyone* (whoever) can be saved. Not all will be saved, but anyone can be saved. God sent Jesus to earth to seek and to save lost people (cf. Luke 19:10). And just as the Father sent Jesus to win the lost, Jesus also sent His disciples to win the lost.

Jesus' Commission in the Book of Acts

The final commission of Jesus is in the Book of Acts. These are the last recorded words from Jesus before He ascended back to Heaven. Just before He departed from His disciples from atop the Mount of Olives outside of Jerusalem, Jesus gave this captivating, compelling commission:

> But you will receive power when the Holy Spirit has come upon you; and you shall be My witnesses both in Jerusalem, and in all Judea and Samaria, and even to the remotest part of the earth. (Acts 1:8)

Here, Jesus stressed that the only power potent enough to make His disciples effective in sharing the Gospel was the power of the Holy Spirit. Just as the Spirit had "come upon" (cf. Luke 1:35; Greek, *eperchomai*) Mary when she supernaturally conceived Jesus, even so the Spirit would "come upon" (*eperchomai*) them. Just as Jesus was formed supernaturally in Mary by the Spirit at the incarnation, Jesus would be formed supernaturally in every believer by the

Spirit at regeneration. Also, the Spirit would empower them supernaturally to be witnesses who would boldly, effectively, and verbally share Jesus with lost people.

The disciples were to begin witnessing right where they were—Jerusalem. They were then to branch out to the surrounding area of Judea. After that, they were to share Jesus with a different ethnic group—the Samaritans, whom the Jewish people despised and discriminated against. Once that barrier was crossed, they would take the Gospel to "the remotest part of the earth," meaning to the Gentiles. The Old Testament Jews were chosen by God, not for privilege, but rather to proclaim His Word to the Gentiles. Now God had chosen these Jewish Christians of the New Testament to share the Gospel with all people, including Gentiles! They were chosen for proclamation, not privilege.

These five commissions are as valid for every Christian today as they were when Jesus gave them in the first century. They accentuate the fact that every Christian has been com-missioned by the Lord Himself to share Jesus with lost people with the intention of winning them to Him!

Challenge:

Jesus has commissioned *you* to share His Gospel with lost people. Will you agree with Him that evangelism (sharing Jesus) is *your* responsibility?

For Memory and Meditation:

"But you will receive power when the Holy Spirit has come upon you; and you shall be My witnesses both in Jerusalem, and in all Judea and Samaria, and even to the remotest part of the earth" (Acts 1:8).

Chapter 3
The Nature of and Need for Salvation

"For by grace you have been saved through faith; and that not of yourselves, it is the gift of God; not as a result of works, so that no one may boast." (Eph. 2:8-9)

Both the nature of salvation and man's need for salvation motivate Christians to share Jesus with lost people. Salvation in Jesus is a glorious, gracious gift provided by God for every person. Salvation enables people to live meaningful lives on earth and assures them eternity with God in Heaven after they die. Let's look at the nature of salvation and man's need for it.

The Nature of Salvation

God is sovereign. He is in complete control. He is above everyone and everything, lofty and exalted, ruling and reigning over the universe. God is omnipotent (all-powerful), omnipresent (all-present), and omniscient (all-knowing). He is eternal, without beginning or end. He is self-sufficient, needing no one or nothing to endure. He created all that exists. He is holy, righteous, and sinless and because he hates sin, He must punish it. Yet this same awesome, imposing, magnificent God is also loving, gracious and merciful toward sinners. He desires all people to be saved and to come to the knowledge of the truth in Jesus Christ.

These biblical facts concerning God explain why the nature of salvation must be by grace, through faith, in Jesus Christ.

Salvation Is by Grace Alone

Salvation is God's gracious gift to man. Man is sinful. He cannot save himself or earn his salvation. Man does not deserve salvation. All humans are born with sinful natures. When we reach the point that we comprehend we are breaking God's laws, we become responsible before God for our sins. We are no longer sinners by nature only, but also sinners by choice.

This is why God must offer salvation by His grace. Grace means that salvation is a gift from God to man. Man is too sinful to earn salvation through good works.

God says through Paul in Ephesians 2:8-9, "For *by grace you have been saved* through faith; and that not of yourselves, *it is the gift of God; not as a result of works, so that no one may boast.*" Salvation is an undeserved gift from God to man, not a payment to man for his religious works. If man could earn his salvation, he would boast about it.

Every other religion apart from Christianity requires man to earn his salvation by working his way up to God. However,

God knew that man could never do that because man is are sinful and God is holy. So, when we could not work our way up to God, He graciously came down to us through His Son, Jesus Christ. Paul said in Titus 3:5, "He saved us, not on the basis of deeds which we have done in righteousness, but according to His mercy, by the washing of regeneration and renewing by the Holy Spirit."

When Jesus came to this earth through the virgin birth, God offered to all sinners His love and forgiveness so He could reconcile them to Himself in salvation by grace alone.

Salvation Is through Faith Alone

The only way sinful man can appropriate and receive the grace of God is through faith. Again, Paul said in Ephesians 2:8-9, "For by grace you have been saved *through faith;* and that not of yourselves, it is the gift of God; not as a result of works, so that no one may boast." Sinful man must trust Jesus to save him. That involves more than assenting intellectually to the facts that Jesus died for sins and rose from the dead. Sinful man must trust that Christ died for *his* sins and rose from the dead to give *him* eternal life.

In his renowned Greek commentary, the late Dr. A.T. Robertson, professor of New Testament interpretation at Southern Baptist Theological Seminary in Louisville, Kentucky, made this astute observation regarding the relationship between grace and faith in salvation based on Paul's words in Ephesians 2:8-9:

For by grace (τη γαρ χαριτι [tēi gar chariti]). Explanatory reason. "By the grace" already mentioned in verse 5 and so with the article. Through faith *(δια πιστεως [dia pisteōs]). This phrase he adds in repeating what he said in verse 5 to make it plainer.* **"Grace" is God's part, "faith" ours.** And that (και τουτο [kai touto]). Neuter, not feminine ταυτη [tautē], and so refers not to πιστις [pistis] (feminine) or to χαρις [charis] (feminine also), but *to the act of being saved by grace conditioned on faith on our part. Paul shows that salvation does not have its source (ἐξ ὑμων [ex humōn], out of you) in men, but from God. Besides, it is God's gift (δωρον [dōron]) and not the result of our work.*[2]

God gives grace, but it is our responsibility to believe in order to be saved. God does not believe for us!

Salvation Is in Jesus Christ Alone

The object of one's faith for salvation is crucial. There is only one way to be saved, and that is through the Lord Jesus Christ. Jesus is not the *best* way to God; He is the *only* way to God. Jesus said in John 14:6, "I am the way, the truth, and the life; no one comes to the Father but through Me." Referring to Jesus, Peter said, "And there is salvation in no one else; for there is no other name under Heaven that has been given among men by which we must be saved" (Acts 4:12). Paul taught in 1 Timothy 2:5, "For there is one God, and one

---
[2] A.T. Robertson, *Word Pictures in the New Testament* (Nashville, TN: Broadman Press, 1933), Eph 2:8. Electronic edition.

mediator also between God and men, the man Christ Jesus." These passages all stress that salvation is in Jesus alone.

Buddha cannot save you. Allah or Mohammed cannot save you. Your religious works cannot save you. Only Jesus can save you. If you don't know Jesus in salvation, you don't know God. If you die without knowing Jesus in salvation, you will spend eternity in Hell, not Heaven.

This brings us to our next emphasis—man's need for salvation.

According to Scripture, why does every man *need* to be saved?

Man Is a Sinner who Needs a Savior

Every person needs to be saved because each of us is a sinner. We have broken God's laws. We are spiritual lawbreakers. Our "sin is lawlessness" (1 John 3:4). We are born with a sinful nature (Ps. 51:5). By nature, we are "children of wrath" (Eph. 2:3). We have a propensity toward sin.

In time we all choose willfully to sin. The Bible says in Isaiah 53:6, "All of us like sheep have gone astray, each of us has turned to his own way." Paul said in Romans 3:23, "For all have sinned and fall short of the glory of God." We are all sinners who need someone else to save us. The only person who qualifies is Jesus.

Man Is Spiritually Dead and Needs Resurrection

The Apostle Paul said in Ephesians 2:1-3:

> *And you were dead in your trespasses and sins, in which you formerly walked according to the course of this world, according to the prince of the power of the air, of the spirit that is now working in the sons of disobedience. Among them we too all formerly lived in the lusts of our flesh, indulging the desires of the flesh and of the mind, and were by nature children of wrath, even as the rest.*

People who do not know Jesus are spiritually "dead" and separated from Him. Paul added that lost people are "separate from Christ, excluded from the commonwealth of Israel, and strangers to the covenants of promise, having no hope and without God in the world" (Eph. 2:12). Lost people need to be raised spiritually from the dead and brought back to Him.

Some interpreted these verses to say that since man is "dead in [his] trespasses and sins," he is like a dead corpse incapable of repenting and believing in Jesus or receiving Him as Savior and Lord. They ask, "After all, how can a dead man repent and believe?" But if Paul meant that lost people are dead corpses incapable of doing anything, then they can't even sin! We ask, "After all, how can a dead corpse sin?"

Paul was not implying that a lost person is a spiritual corpse incapable of responding to God in repentance and faith. The text itself shows that those who were spiritually dead were still active. They *walked* in accordance with this sinful world (v. 2), *lived* in the lusts of their flesh, and *indulged* their flesh (v. 3). Dead corpses cannot walk, live, or indulge.

Paul's phrase "dead in trespasses and sins" simply emphasizes the fact that sin separates man from God (Isa. 59:1-2). Anyone outside of Christ is dead in sin and separated from God. He needs to receive eternal life from Jesus, who is "the way, and the truth, and the life" (John 14:6).

Man Is Spiritually Sick and Needs a Physician

Being "dead in sin" is not the only (or primary) example used in Scripture to describe lost people. Jesus also said that lost people are *spiritually sick*. Incidentally, the question mentioned above, "How can a dead man repent and believe?" becomes irrelevant when facing this example. No one in his right mind would ask, "How can a sick man repent and believe?" Yet Jesus referred to lost people as being spiritually sick.

The Jewish religious leaders of Jesus' day did not appreciate the fact that Jesus associated with tax collectors, prostitutes, and other "sinners." When they confronted Him in this regard, Jesus replied with this powerful statement: "It is not those who are healthy who need a physician, but those who are sick; I did not come to call the righteous, but sinners" (Mark 2:17). People are sinners and they are spiritually sick. We all need to be healed spiritually with the salvation that only Jesus, our Great Physician, can offer.

Man Is a Spiritual Slave and Needs a Liberator

Some of the Jewish religious leaders of Jesus' day supposedly believed in Him for salvation. But when Jesus spoke further to them, they became highly offended:

So Jesus was saying to those Jews who had believed Him,

If you continue in My word, then you are truly disciples of Mine; and you will know the truth, and the truth will make you free." They answered Him, "We are Abraham's descendants and have never yet been enslaved to anyone; how is it that You say, 'You will become free'?" Jesus answered them, "Truly, truly, I say to you, everyone who commits sin is the slave of sin. The slave does not remain in the house forever; the son does remain forever. So if the Son makes you free, you will be free indeed (John 8:31-36).

Anyone who did not know Jesus in salvation was a slave to sin in need of a Savior who could liberate him from his iniquity. When non-Christians in our day come to Jesus in repentance and faith, He sets them free spiritually.

Man Is a Rebel that Needs a Master (Lord)

The first man and His wife, Adam and Eve, rebelled against God and ate fruit that God had forbidden them to eat. That rebellious act opened the door for the curse of sin to infect the entire universe, including the heart of every human being who would ever live. Thus, at conception, we inherit Adam's rebellious, sinful nature. We are spiritual rebels by birth and eventually by choice. We need the Master, the Lord Jesus Christ, to conquer our rebellious hearts and bring His order back into our lives.

Paul explains how that happens in Romans 10:9-10, "That if you confess with your mouth Jesus as Lord, and believe in your heart that God raised Him from the dead, you will be saved; for with the heart a person believes, resulting in righteousness, and with the mouth he confesses, resulting in salvation." The moment you believe savingly in Jesus, He transforms you from a rebel into His loyal servant. Jesus becomes your Master and Lord.

Challenge:

Are you able to articulate the nature of salvation with others? Can you explain to non-Christians why salvation is by grace alone, through faith alone, and in Christ alone? Do you also recognize what the Bible teaches about all people needing salvation?

For Memory and Meditation:

"For by grace you have been saved through faith; and that not of yourselves, it is the gift of God; not as a result of works, so that no one may boast" (Eph. 2:8-9).

Chapter 4
The Three Components of Salvation

"How will we escape if we neglect so great a salvation?" (Heb. 2:3)

As the writer of Hebrews says, redemption in Jesus Christ is a "great" salvation. Why is that? Exactly what does a person obtain when he receives salvation? According to Scripture, salvation in Jesus has three components. First, we enter into a relationship with God through Christ when we are born again by His Spirit. That is *regeneration*. Second, we begin to grow and mature in grace and in the knowledge and likeness of Jesus. That is *sanctification*. Then, the moment we die, our spirit and soul leave our body and go to be with Jesus in Heaven. That is *glorification*. Anyone who becomes a Christian experiences all three of these components of salvation.

Regeneration: Being Born Again

One night a leading Pharisee named Nicodemus came to discuss Jesus' teachings with Him. He said to Jesus, "Rabbi, we know that You have come from God as a teacher; for no one can do these signs that You do unless God is with him" (John 3:2). But Jesus immediately changed the direction of the conversation with this terse response, "Truly, truly, I say to you, unless one is born again he cannot see the kingdom of God" (v. 3).

To be "born again" is to be "born of the Spirit" (vv. 5-8) and is the first component of salvation. Theologians refer to it as regeneration. Regeneration occurs the moment a person repents of his sin, believes in Jesus' atoning death and bodily resurrection, and receives Jesus as Savior and Lord by willfully calling on His name.

Regeneration Is Instantaneous. Regeneration is punctiliar. It happens at a specific point in time and then continues with an abiding result. One second a person is lost and on his way to Hell, but then he repents, believes, and receives Jesus, and he is immediately saved. No one has *always* been saved. Rather, regeneration occurs the moment one repents of sin, believes savingly in Jesus, and receives Him as Savior and Lord.

Regeneration Is Like Being Born. Jesus said, "Truly, truly, I say to you, unless one is born of water and the Spirit he cannot enter into the kingdom of God. That which is born of the flesh is flesh, and that which is born of the Spirit is spirit. Do not be amazed that I said to you, 'You must be born again'" (John 3:5-7). A child is born at a specific time on a specific day. That is the way people are saved. We are regenerated by the Holy Spirit at a specific time on a specific day. Thus, when He saved or regenerated Zacchaeus, Jesus said, "Today salvation has come to this house" (Luke 19:9). Regeneration happens at a moment of time and then abides forever.

Regeneration Is Like Getting Married. Regeneration is actually a spiritual wedding. Referring to the salvation of the Corinthians, Paul said, "For I am jealous for you with the jealousy of God himself. I promised you as a pure bride to one husband—Christ" (2 Cor. 11:2 NLT). Jesus is pictured as the groom at a wedding, and Christians are pictured as the bride. Regeneration is like being married to our beloved groom, Jesus! Again, it happens at a moment of time and then abides forever.

Regeneration Is Like Becoming a Disciple or Student. Jesus said in the Great Commission, "Go therefore and make *disciples* of all the nations" (Matt. 28:19a). When a disciple is made, that means he is born again "by the washing of regeneration and renewing by the Holy Spirit" (Titus 3:5). When someone becomes a Christian, he becomes a student/ follower/disciple of the greatest Teacher ever to live—Jesus.

Regeneration Is Like Putting on Clothes. In the Old Testament, God promised to clothe His people in His righteousness. The prophet Isaiah referred to this when he said,

> *I will rejoice greatly in the LORD,*
> *My soul will exult in my God;*
> *For He has clothed me with garments of salvation,*
> *He has wrapped me with a robe of righteousness,*
> *As a bridegroom decks himself with a garland,*
> *And as a bride adorns herself with her jewels"*
> *(Isa. 61:10).*

Likewise, the Apostle Paul encouraged new Christians by saying, "For all of you who were baptized into Christ have clothed yourselves with Christ" (Gal. 3:27). To be baptized into Christ means to be born again—regenerated—and thus clothed with Christ.

Has there ever been a specific point in time when you willfully repented of your sin, believed that Jesus died and rose from the dead to save you, and received Him into your heart as your Lord and Savior? If so, that is when you were born again. That is when you were regenerated!

Sanctification: Becoming More Like Jesus

The moment a person is saved and regenerated, he is immediately set apart by God to grow in grace and become more like Jesus, which is the ultimate goal of the Christian life. This is called sanctification.

Sanctification Begins at Regeneration. The split second a person repents of his sin, believes savingly in Jesus, and receives Jesus as Lord and Savior, God sets him apart from other people to be His. A person is literally made into a "saint" (set apart one) the moment he gets saved.

When Paul wrote to the Christians at Corinth, he set forth a long list of sins. Those sins, if practiced perpetually as a person's lifestyle, indicated that person was not a real Christian. But immediately following that list, Paul made this amazing statement: "Such *were* some of you; but you were *washed*, but you were *sanctified*, but you were *justified* in the name of the Lord Jesus Christ and in the Spirit of our God" (1 Cor. 6:11). Many of the Christians at Corinth had committed these sins before regeneration. But the split second they became a Christian, they were "washed… sanctified… [set apart]… justified" by Jesus. The initial part of sanctification means that God sets believers in Jesus apart from all other people to be His.

Sanctification Continues throughout One's Earthly Life. Regeneration, which includes the initial act of sanctification, results in a lifetime of growing and maturing in Christlikeness. The fact that a person is becoming more and more like Jesus as time passes is a sure indicator that his conversion was real. Jesus said, "You will know them [Christians] by their fruits" (Matt. 7:20). Thus, in order to go to Heaven you must be genuinely born again, and the proof of salvation is the display of Christlike "fruit" in your life. That is exactly why the author of Hebrews urged, "Pursue peace with all men, and *the sanctification without which no one will see the Lord*" (Heb. 12:14). If there is no spiritual fruit, then there is no spiritual root. Where there is fruit, that is indicative of one rooted in Jesus. Then for the rest of your life you will grow in grace.

God Sanctifies by Teaching Us. Jesus matures us in Christlikeness by teaching us through the truth of His written Word—the Bible. The Holy Spirit takes the Bible that He inspired and teaches us how to be conformed to the image of Jesus. That's why Jesus said, "But the Helper, the Holy Spirit, whom the Father will send in My name, He will teach you all things, and bring to your remembrance all that I said to you" (John 14:26).

God Sanctifies by Testing Us. God never tempts us to sin, but He does test us to sanctify and purify us (Gen. 22:1f). The Bible says in Proverbs 17:3, "The refining pot is for silver and the furnace for gold, but the LORD tests hearts." God tests us to refine us like silver and gold. He removes the impurities from us through the tests He allows into our lives.

James, the brother of Jesus, said we should actually rejoice when we fall into tests and trials. Why? Because God uses them to mature us. James said, "Consider it all joy, my brethren, when you encounter various trials, knowing that the testing of your faith produces endurance. And let endurance have its perfect result, so that you may be perfect and complete, lacking in nothing" (James 1:2-4).

God Sanctifies by Pruning Us. Similar to testing us, God also "prunes" us. Jesus is the Vine and we are the branches. We must abide in Him if we desire to be fruitful. And when we produce spiritual fruit, Jesus "prunes" us like a gardener prunes a plant or tree to make it produce even more in the days ahead. Jesus said in John 15:2, "Every branch in Me that does not bear fruit, He takes away; and every branch that bears fruit, He prunes it so that it may bear more fruit." Pruning is not punishment, although it might feel uncomfortable at the time. It is actually a reward from Jesus to help us become even more fruitful in His work.

God Sanctifies by Disciplining Us. Unlike many modern parents, when God's children disobey Him, he spanks them!

God always disciplines His wayward children. He does it, not because He hates them, but because He loves them too much to allow them to sin without being corrected. Jesus said these strong words to admonish the sinful Christians at the church of Laodicea, "Those whom I love, I reprove and discipline; therefore be zealous and repent" (Rev. 3:19). If someone sins and is not disciplined by God, it is a strong indicator that he is not a genuine Christian (cf. Heb. 12:8). God disciplines His disobedient children so they can "share His holiness" (Heb. 12:10).

Sanctification is when God sets you apart at regeneration and then conforms you into the image of Jesus throughout the rest of your life on earth.

Glorification: Beholding Jesus in Heaven

Should Jesus delay His return to earth, you and I will experience physical death. That will be the day when our sanctification process is complete. Paul said, "He who began a good work in you will perfect it until the day of Christ Jesus" (Phil. 1:6). God, who began His "good work" of salvation in you at regeneration, continues it in sanctification, and will perfect it one day at the moment of glorification—when you see Jesus!

The Bible teaches that at death both the soul and spirit of a Christian immediately go to be with the Lord. That is when the believer enters into the eternal state of glorification. Paul referred to glorification when he said, "We are confident, I say, and willing rather to be absent from the body, and to be present with the Lord" (2 Cor. 5:8 KJV). The second a Christian dies, his soul and spirit leave his body and go to be with Jesus in Heaven. No wonder Jesus said to the repentant thief who was about to die on the cross, "Truly I say to you, *today* you shall be with Me in Paradise" (Luke 23:43).

The moment we see Jesus after we have died and gone to Heaven, He will complete His saving work in us. We are robed in Jesus' righteousness at regeneration (Isa. 61:10; 2 Cor. 5:21). We also walk in "paths of righteousness" during the process of sanctification (Ps. 23:3). Then finally, at glorification, Jesus will reward us with the crown of righteousness to go along with our robe of righteousness. Paul said in 2 Timothy 4:8, "In the future there is laid up for me the crown of righteousness, which the Lord, the righteous Judge, will award to me on that day; and not only to me, but also to all who have loved His appearing." The psalmist looked forward to the day when he would experience glorification and said, "As for me, I shall behold Your face in righteousness; I will be satisfied with Your likeness when I awake" (Ps. 17:15).

One of the greatest blessings of glorification is that when we see Jesus, immediately we will become perfectly like Him. The Apostle John said in 1 John 3:2, "Beloved, now we are children of God, and it has not appeared as yet what we will be. We know that when He appears, we will be like Him, because we will see Him just as He is." An old hymn affirms this by saying, "O that will be *glory* for me… when by His grace I shall look on His face, that will be *glory*, be *glory* for me!"

Challenge:

These three components of salvation show us how wonderful and glorious salvation is. Jesus redeems us at regeneration, matures us through sanctification, and perfects us at glorification. Shouldn't this motivate you to share the Gospel with lost people so they, too, can experience salvation in Jesus in all its amazing components?

For Memory and Meditation:

"How will we escape if we neglect so great a salvation?" (Heb. 2:3)

Chapter 5
The Requirements for Salvation

"He said, 'Sirs, what must I do to be
saved?' They said, 'Believe in the Lord
Jesus, and you will be saved, you and
your household.'" (Acts 16:30b-31)

Paul and Silas were in prison for preaching the Gospel in the
city of Philippi. They had been beaten severely in public and
locked in a dungeon. But at midnight, they began singing
praises to God. The other inmates were listening, and so was
the Lord, Who then sent an earthquake. All the prisoners'
chains fell off, and the prison doors opened. Thinking that the
prisoners had escaped, the jailer was on the verge of taking
his own life, but Paul told him that none of the prisoners had
attempted to escape. Then the jailer asked one of the most
significant questions anyone could ever ask. He fell at Paul's
feet and asked, "Sirs, what must I do to be saved?"

What a great question! What does a person have to do
to become a Christian? What is man's responsibility when it
comes to salvation? Do we just wait for God to sovereignly
"zap" us with eternal life? Does everybody have the same
opportunity to respond and receive God's gift of salvation?

The Bible teaches that salvation is a gift from God. It also
teaches that salvation is a gift that must be received by man.
Giving salvation is God's part; receiving salvation is our part.

38

To be sure, God initiates salvation. He does so by wooing, persuading, and drawing all people to Himself (cf. John 12:32). But in order to be saved, we must respond willfully.

In order to be saved you must: (1) *repent* of your sin, (2) *believe* that Jesus died for your sins and rose from the dead to give you eternal life, and (3) *receive* Jesus as your Savior and Lord.

You Must *Repent* of Your Sin

As we learned in previous chapters, a person cannot experience regeneration (be born again) unless he first repents. To repent is to turn. The Lord helps a sinner turn from his sinful, selfish way of living and turn toward God. Repentance is a change of mind and heart that results in a change of action. It is a spiritual "U-turn," a spiritual "about-face," a spiritual "180."

To be saved, in addition to believing in Jesus, you must also repent. Jesus taught that unless we repent, we will perish (i.e., go to Hell). He said in Luke 13:3, "I tell you, no, but unless you repent, you will all likewise perish." That *all* means *all*, and that's all it means. When Peter proclaimed the Gospel outside the temple, he told his listeners if they wanted to be saved, they had to come to God through Jesus by repenting of their sins. Peter declared in Acts 3:19-20, "Therefore repent and return, so that your sins may be wiped away, in order that times of refreshing may come from the presence of the Lord; and that He may send Jesus, the Christ appointed for you."

This text also shows that God does not regenerate you in order to enable you to repent. The text does *not* say, "Have your sins wiped away, and then you can repent." It says just the opposite: "repent and return, so that your sins may be wiped away." Repentance comes *before* regeneration. That is not "works" salvation, it's biblical theology. We repent, and *then* God wipes away our sins with the cleansing blood of Jesus.

And who can repent? Anyone! That has to be true because God commands *all* people to repent. Paul said in Acts 17:30, "Therefore having overlooked the times of ignorance, God is now declaring to men that all people everywhere should repent." If God commands "all people everywhere" to repent, then anyone can do so. All will not repent, but repentance is open to everyone.

Some people say that even though God commands all people to repent, He only grants repentance to His chosen ones, the elect. However, that would mean that God commands people to repent whom He has already predestined not to repent. If God commands them to repent, yet they are not actually able to because He has not granted them repentance, then they are not responsible. God cannot hold a person responsible for something if that person is not capable of responding. This positions God as acting against Himself, and we know that God cannot be against God. The fact that He commands "all people everywhere" to repent means that everyone everywhere ought to repent, and if they ought to repent, then they can. "Ought" implies "can."

This deals with man's responsibility regarding salvation. The word *responsible* means "able to respond." If you are not really able to respond because God has predestined you not to respond, then you are not responsible. Again, God does not contradict Himself. If He commands you to repent, then you are capable of repenting. That is, you are "responsible" and able to respond.

Repentance must be prominent in any biblical Gospel presentation, because, before anyone can become a Christian, he must repent and turn from his sins.

You Must *Believe* in Jesus

Just as God does not regenerate us so we can repent, God does not regenerate us so we can believe in Him. Instead, the opposite is true. We believe and then we are regenerated by Him.

To believe savingly in Jesus is more than exercising mere "head knowledge." The Bible assures us that even demons believe that Jesus exists, but they are not going to Heaven (James 2:19). Rather, to believe savingly in Jesus means to trust that what He has done redemptively on the cross and in His bodily resurrection is totally sufficient to redeem anyone from the guilt and penalty of his sins. To believe savingly in Jesus is to transfer our trust from ourselves and our good works to what Jesus has already done for us at the cross and at the empty tomb.

Jesus stressed that we must believe if we want to be saved. We read in John 3:16, "For God so loved the world, that

He gave His only begotten Son, that whoever believes in Him shall not perish, but have eternal life." Notice that God loves everyone in the world with the same kind of saving love. He does not want anyone in the world to perish and go to Hell by rejecting Him. Thus, *whoever* believes savingly in Jesus will be saved.

Looking at our original text above, Acts 16:30-31, the Philippian jailer asked Paul what the requirements were for salvation. Paul did not say, "Jesus will save you, and then you can believe." Rather, Paul told Him to believe in Jesus and he would be saved. We read, "And after he brought them out, he said, 'Sirs, what must I do to be saved?' They said, 'Believe in the Lord Jesus, and you will be saved, you and your household.'" That is when the jailer and all the members of his household experienced regeneration by repenting of their sins and believing in Jesus.

This was also Paul's message. He told the Romans that believing in Jesus is essential for regeneration. He said in Romans 10:9-10, "That if you confess with your mouth Jesus as Lord, and *believe in your heart* that God raised Him from the dead, you will be saved; for *with the heart a person believes, resulting in righteousness*, and with the mouth he confesses, resulting in salvation."

To be saved you must believe "in your heart," the center of your mental and spiritual nature. This is where the concept of "asking Jesus into your heart" comes from. Paul says in Romans 10:10 that when someone believes in Jesus with all his heart, he is regenerated and receives the perfect "righteousness" of Jesus.

All of this is experienced through faith. When we believe that Jesus died for *us* and rose from the dead to give *us* eternal life, then we are saved. "By grace you have been saved *through faith*" (Eph. 2:8).

The writer of Hebrews said, "Without faith it is impossible to please Him, for he who comes to God *must believe* that He is and that He is a rewarder of those who seek Him" (Heb. 11:6). Faith in Jesus is essential for regeneration and also for continued sanctification. Before you can become a Christian, you must believe savingly in Jesus Christ.

You Must *Receive* Jesus as Lord and Savior

A person cannot be born again (regenerated) unless he first receives Jesus as Lord and Savior. To receive Jesus means to accept Him. "Receive" is the Greek word *lambano*. It means to "accept, invite." At a specific moment in time, you volitionally invite Jesus Christ to come into your life to be your Savior and Lord.

The Apostle John says in John 1:12, "But as many as *received* Him, to them He gave the right to become children of God, even to those who believe in His name." Notice that *receiving* Jesus is connected with *believing* in His name. All of these—repentance, believing, and receiving are prerequisites to regeneration, not products of it.

The Apostle Paul said that the Gospel he preached was something that his listeners needed to "receive." He said in 1 Corinthians 15:1-2, "Now I make known to you, brethren, the gospel which I preached to you, which also you *received*, in which also you stand, by which also you are saved, if you hold fast the word which I preached to you, unless you believed in vain." Paul shared Jesus by preaching the Gospel, and as a result many people responded by receiving Jesus as Savior and Lord.

Again, receiving Jesus is not a meritorious "work." If a person offers a piece of bread to a hungry person, the hungry person must receive the offered gift before he can enjoy it. When he accepts that bread, he isn't working for it; he's merely receiving it. Even so, God offers salvation to needy spiritual "beggars" that must receive the Bread of Life—Jesus (John 6:35).

God offers salvation to all and gives all the freedom to accept it or reject it. He never forces salvation on anyone. He does not "bend the will" of anyone. "Forced love" is against the law of man and also against the law of God, and with good reason. Forced love is not real love. Rather, it is a violation of love. For love to be legitimate, it must be both genuinely offered and willfully received.

No one has to receive Jesus. Anyone can say "no" to God. When He offers us salvation by wooing, persuading, and drawing us to Him, we can resist His overtures of grace (Acts 7:51).

The Bible says that Jesus "felt a love" for the rich, young ruler. Jesus obviously wanted to save him. He offered him the opportunity to follow Him as His disciple. But the rich, young ruler said, "No!" He rejected Jesus' invitation to follow Him and "he went away" lost (Mark 10:21f).

Jesus also desired to save lost people in Jerusalem. He said He longed to gather them together "the way a hen gathers her chicks under her wings," but He did not because they rejected His offer. He did not give them salvation because they were unwilling (Matt. 23:37).

Likewise, when Jesus went to His hometown of Nazareth, he "could not" do many miracles there, with the exception of healing a few sick people. Why? Because of *their* unbelief! Their lack of faith caused Jesus not to save them. It also caused Him to marvel (Mark 6:5-6).

God offers salvation to all people and they can either receive Jesus as Lord and Savior by means of repenting and believing, or they can reject Jesus' offer to be saved and suffer the consequences.

Challenge:

Have you met God's requirements for salvation? Have you: (1) repented and turned from your selfish, sinful way of living; (2) believed savingly in Jesus, trusting that His atoning death and bodily resurrection are absolutely sufficient to pay your sin debt; and (3) received Jesus as your Lord and Savior by calling on His name in prayer? If not, will you do that this very moment? If you have, will you start sharing Jesus with lost people?

For Memory and Meditation:

"He said, 'Sirs, what must I do to be saved?' They said, 'Believe in the Lord Jesus, and you will be saved, you and your household'" (Acts 16:30b-31).

Chapter 6
The Assurance and Permanence of Salvation: "Once Saved, Always Saved"

"These things I have written to you who believe in the name of the Son of God, so that you may know that you have eternal life." (1 John 5:13)

The Apostle John told his readers that he had written his first letter to people who had believed in Jesus so they would know for certain they had eternal life. He wanted them to have assurance of their salvation.

Is it possible for someone to *know* he is a Christian? Can someone know without a doubt that he has a home in Heaven and when he dies he will live there forever? Or is it possible for a Christian to lose his salvation? Can a Christian somehow forfeit his relationship with Christ and not go to Heaven when he dies?

The Bible teaches that those who have been genuinely saved in Jesus Christ can know for certain that they are saved and that they are on their way to Heaven. The Bible also teaches that once a person becomes a child of God in salvation, he will *always* be a child of God. You cannot "lose" your salvation. If you are genuinely saved, you will *always* be saved.

Assurance of Salvation—Can I Know I Am Saved?

Years ago I heard a person pray this prayer: "Lord, save us all in Heaven." Her denomination believed that no Christian can know for certain that he is saved and on his way to Heaven. Instead, the best anyone can do is to hope he lives "good enough" so that one day God will save him in Heaven.

I'm so glad the Bible doesn't teach that! I'm grateful I can *know* I am saved right now. I have a "know-so" salvation, not a "hope-so" salvation. The Bible teaches that (1) we can know we are saved, and (2) once we are saved we remain saved forever.

Yet, many Christians often ask questions like these: "How can I know I am really saved?" "Is my salvation based on the way I feel?" "Is there any chance I could lose my salvation?" "How can I be certain that I will go to Heaven?"

Jesus said in John 5:24, "Truly, truly, I say to you, he who hears My word, and believes Him who sent Me, has eternal life, and does not come into judgment, but has passed out of death into life." Jesus was saying that when a person "believes" and trusts savingly in Jesus, he receives "eternal life." He "has" it immediately and permanently. It is a certain, knowable fact. Eternal life belongs to him as a free gift from God. Because Jesus says he has it, he does not have to wonder if he has it. Note also that it is *eternal* life. It is both life on a higher plain (i.e., abundant life, John 10:10) and also everlasting life, meaning that the person will live with God in Heaven forever (John 6:51, 58).

The Apostle Paul also taught that Christians can be certain they are saved and en route to Heaven. He said, "I *know* whom I have believed, and am persuaded that he is able to keep that which I have committed unto him against that day" (2 Tim. 1:12b KJV). Paul *knew* he had believed in the Lord. That caused him to be confidently persuaded that Jesus Christ was alive and able to keep, (guard, watch over) his soul which he had committed to Him at regeneration.

John the Apostle also wrote about the assurance of one's salvation when he said, "These things I have written to you who believe in the name of the Son of God, so *that you may know that you have eternal life*" (1 John 5:13). The word "know" means that we can be absolutely certain we are saved.

This was a favorite verse of my mentor in evangelism, Dr. Roy Fish, former professor of evangelism at Southwestern Baptist Theological Seminary in Fort Worth, Texas. In fact, Dr. Fish requested that at the viewing of his body prior to his funeral, his Bible would be open in his hand with his index finger pointing to 1 John 5:13! Just like Abel, though he was dead, he still spoke (Heb. 11:4). Dr. Fish wanted everyone to know, even after his death, that Christians can be assured of their salvation!

So how can we know we are saved? What are the biblical signs of salvation?

Biblical Indicators of Salvation

You can know you're saved because the Bible says so. The Bible is God's Word. God is holy and perfect and cannot lie. Consequently, every word in God's Word, the Bible, is true. When it comes to the subject of being saved, the Bible clearly states that whoever repents of his sin, believes on the Lord Jesus, and receives Him into his life, has the gift of salvation.

The Apostle John affirmed this when he said, "But as many as received Him, to them He gave the right to become children of God, even to those who believe in His name" (John 1:12). That is, if you receive Christ and believe savingly in His name, then Jesus gives you the right to become a child of God! Jesus said, "Truly, truly, I say to you, he who believes has eternal life" (John 6:47). Thus, if a person believes savingly in Jesus, eternal life is the inevitable result. Paul, too, affirmed this by saying, "For "Whoever will call on the name of the Lord *will be saved*" (Rom. 10:13). He did not say, "*might* be saved." He said that if you call on the Lord's name for salvation, you "*will* be saved." The Bible teaches that if you have sincerely repented, believed, and received, you are saved!

You know you're saved when you love other Christians. When you become a Christian, God places His love for others within you. When as a college student I began following Jesus, I immediately began to love and enjoy being around people that I would have never associated with beforehand. Prior to that, I would have never fraternized with anyone who was not athletic, sharp looking, or "cool." But God supernaturally put His love for all Christians in my heart.

Paul affirms this by saying, "The love of God has been poured out within our hearts through the Holy Spirit who was given to us" (Rom. 5:5). Every Christian in the world becomes your brother or sister in Christ. When God saves you, He gives you a genuine love for all other Christians. The Apostle John affirmed this when he wrote, "We know that we have passed out of death into life, *because we love the brethren. He who does not love abides in death"* (1 John 3:14). Love for other Christians is a sure sign that a person possesses salvation in Jesus.

You know you're saved when you sense the presence of the Holy Spirit. The moment you become a Christian, God sends His Holy Spirit to live within your physical body. Your body literally becomes "a temple of the Holy Spirit" (1 Cor. 6:19). Paul tells us we can know we are saved because, "the Spirit Himself testifies with our spirit that we are children of God" (Rom. 8:16). That is, God's Holy Spirit speaks to us deep in our hearts and tells us we are God's children. The Spirit within causes you to have an overwhelming realization that God has regenerated and transformed you into a new creation, and that you now belong to Jesus.

You know you're saved when you desire to obey God. When you become a Christian you do not become perfect. But you do become God's child, and you do begin to desire to obey God and do what He says. That is why John said, "And we can be sure that we know him if we obey his commandments." (1 John 2:3 NLT). When you get saved, you begin to enjoy obeying God instead of disobeying God. Such a change in your joy is an assuring sign that you have been saved.

You know you're saved when you desire to read your Bible. Salvation results in a desire to read and study God's Word, the Bible. A child of God will desire to know what his Heavenly Father says. Peter noted this when he said, "Like newborn babies, long for the pure milk of the word, so that by it you may grow in respect to salvation, if you have tasted the kindness of the Lord" (1 Pet. 2:2-3). A new Christian will hunger for God's Word like a baby craves milk. A hunger for the Word of God assures you that the God of the Word has saved you!

You know you're saved when you experience answered prayers. When you receive the gift of salvation, God begins to answer your prayers. Jesus said, "If you abide in Me, and My words abide in you, ask whatever you wish, and it will be done for you" (John 15:7). When we pray according to His will, God hears our prayers and promises to answer them (1 John 5:14-15). God does not always answer our prayers by saying, "yes." He might say "no," or "wait." Nevertheless, He always answers our prayers according to His perfect will.

These are some of the ways that you can "test" yourself (2 Cor. 13:5) to be assured and know you are saved. But how can you be sure that once you are saved, you won't lose or forfeit your salvation?

Three Reasons You Will Not "Lose" Your Salvation

Nothing can separate you from the Father's love. God loves you with "an everlasting love" (Jer. 31:3). Paul penned the Lord's guarantee that nothing will ever disconnect a Christian from God's love. He wrote, "For I am convinced that neither death, nor life, nor angels, nor principalities, nor things present, nor things to come, nor powers, nor height, nor depth, nor any other created thing, will be able to separate us from the love of God, which is in Christ Jesus our Lord" (Rom. 8:38-39). God's saving love for every believer is an *everlasting* love!

No one can snatch you from the Son's hand. Jesus said, "My sheep hear My voice, and I know them, and they follow Me; and I give eternal life to them, and they will never perish; and *no one will snatch them out of My hand.* My Father, who has given them to Me, is greater than all; and no one is able to snatch them out of the Father's hand" (John 10:27-29). When you become a Christian, God puts an eternal "hold" on you. Your salvation does not depend on your being able to hold on to God. Rather, your salvation continues eternally because God is holding on to you! Jesus illustrates that you are "under double-lock-and-key." Jesus holds you with His hands, and God the Father also holds you with His hands. Thus, to steal your salvation, the devil would have to pry open the hands of both Jesus and God the Father to snatch you away. You can rest assured that will *never* happen!

Nothing can sever you from the Spirit's seal. When God saved you, He "sealed" your salvation with His Holy Spirit. The

Bible says, "In Him, you also, after listening to the message of truth, the gospel of your salvation—having also believed, you were sealed in Him with the Holy Spirit of promise, who is given as a pledge of our inheritance, with a view to the redemption of God's own possession, to the praise of His glory" (Eph. 1:13-14). The seal of God's Spirit acts literally as a binding "pledge," a spiritual down payment that guarantees the completion of the reward of salvation in Heaven. The Spirit's seal cannot be severed or broken by anyone or anything. Thus, our salvation is absolutely secure!

Challenge:

If you have: (1) repented of your sin, (2) believed that Jesus died for you and rose from the dead for you, and (3) received Jesus into your life by asking Him to save you, then rest assured He has done just that. You are saved because the Bible says so. Take a moment and pray this simple prayer: "Thank You, dear Father, that I *know* I am saved!"

For Memory and Meditation:

"These things I have written to you who believe in the name of the Son of God, so that you may know that you have eternal life" (1 John 5:13).

Chapter 7
Identify and Pray for Lost People

"Brethren, my heart's desire and my prayer to God for them is for their salvation." (Rom. 10:1)

How exactly can we share Jesus with people who do not know Him as Savior and Lord in a biblical, polite, competent manner? According to Jesus, most people are lost and need to be saved:

> *Enter through the narrow gate; for the gate is wide and the way is broad that leads to destruction, and there are many who enter through it. For the gate is small and the way is narrow that leads to life, and there are few who find it (Matt. 7:13-14).*

Jesus was saying that the majority of people don't enter the narrow, small gate (Jesus) or walk on the narrow way that leads to everlasting life (Heaven). Instead, most people enter the wide gate and walk on the broad road in life (a life without Jesus) and spend eternity in "destruction" (Hell). That truth should motivate Christians to share Jesus with lost people.

But how do we identify lost people? If most people are without Christ, then lost people are all around us. Who are they, and how can we recognize them?

Identifying Lost People

When I went to Southwestern Baptist Theological Seminary in 1980, one of the Evangelism professors had just died. His name was Oscar Thompson. Dr. Thompson was writing a book entitled, *Concentric Circles of Concern*.[3] After his death, his wife, Carolyn, helped complete his work in 1981. In that book, the Thompson gave seven strategic, "concentric circles" of relationships that help any believer discover lost people with whom they can share Jesus.

Moving from the innermost circle of one's "self" to the outermost circle of a person whom we have never met (person "X"), those concentric circles are: (1) self; (2) immediate family; (3) relatives; (4) close friends; (5) neighbors and business associates; (6) acquaintances; and (7) person "X."

Circle 1—Self. The soul-winner who shares Jesus with lost people must make sure that he himself is saved. It would be a tragedy for someone to tell others how to know Jesus in salvation, only to discover at the end of life that he is not a genuine follower of Christ.

You might say, "That could never happen. Anyone who tells others about Jesus must be saved." But the Bible clearly

---

[3] W. Oscar Thompson, *Concentric Circles of Concern* (Nashville: Broadman Press, 1981).

teaches that on the day of final judgment, many who think they are saved and en route to Heaven will discover they are not saved and are on their way to Hell.

Jesus said in Matthew 7:21-23, "Not everyone who says to Me, 'Lord, Lord,' will enter the kingdom of heaven, but he who does the will of My Father who is in Heaven will enter. Many will say to Me on that day, 'Lord, Lord, did we not prophesy in Your name, and in Your name cast out demons, and in Your name perform many miracles?' And then I will declare to them, 'I never knew you; Depart from Me, you who practice lawlessness.'" According to Jesus, "many" will think they are saved only to discover at the final judgment that they are lost! How dreadful!

Paul urged us to test and examine ourselves to see if we are really saved. He says in 2 Corinthians 13:5, "Test yourselves to see if you are in the faith; examine yourselves! Or do you not recognize this about yourselves, that Jesus Christ is in you—unless indeed you fail the test?"

In chapter 6, we looked at several biblical indicators that assure a person of salvation.

1. You know you're saved because the Bible says so. The Bible clearly states that whoever repents, believes in Jesus, and receives Him is saved.

2. You know you're saved when you love other Christians.

3. You know you're saved when you sense the presence of the Holy Spirit in your life.

4. You know you're saved when you desire to obey God.
5. You know you're saved when you desire to read Your Bible.
6. You know you're saved when you experience answered prayers.

These tests help you discern whether or not you are saved.

Circle 2—Immediate Family. Most everyone has immediate family members who are lost. Perhaps your spouse is not a Christian. Maybe your children have grown into their teenage years and have not yet trusted Christ as Savior. Maybe your parents or siblings are not saved.

As soon as Andrew became a follower of Jesus, he introduced his brother, Simon (Peter), to Jesus (John 1:35-42). Likewise, when the Philippian jailer received Jesus as Savior, he made sure his family also came to faith in Christ (Acts 16:34).

Circle 3—Relatives. Just as people have immediate family members who are lost, they also have extended family members—uncles, aunts, grandparents, grandchildren, nieces, nephews, cousins, and so forth—who are without Christ and need to hear the Gospel.

Years ago my wife began to pray for several of her relatives who did not know Jesus. She felt led to pray especially for one of her uncles who lived far from us. Within a year, he accepted Jesus as his Savior and Lord. I'm convinced that my wife's prayers helped to cultivate the soil of his heart so the seed of the Gospel could bear good fruit (Matt. 13:8, 23).

Circle 4—Friends. Do all of your friends know Jesus as Lord and Savior? One of the most sincere ways of being a good friend is to share Jesus with someone who is lost. It should be natural, especially since that person is someone with whom you already have a connection.

Paul loved his Jewish friends and wanted them to be saved. He said in Romans 9:1-4a, "I am telling the truth in Christ, I am not lying, my conscience testifies with me in the Holy Spirit, that I have great sorrow and unceasing grief in my heart. For I could wish that I myself were accursed, separated from Christ for the sake of my brethren, my kinsmen according to the flesh, who are Israelites." Paul was willing to forfeit his own salvation (be "accursed, separated from Christ") if his Jewish friends would come to Christ! Now *that* is being a real friend!

Circle 5—Neighbors and Business Associates. Our neighbors, coworkers, and classmates provide excellent witnessing opportunities. My mentor in prayer, Don Miller of Fort Worth, Texas, once told me that every Christian should use the acronym, "N.E.W.S." to share Jesus with his neighbors. It stands for "North, East, West, and South." Every believer should get to know his neighbors to the north, east, west and south of his home, pray for them, and ask the Lord to give him the opportunity to witness to them.

The same applies to business associates. When I was in seminary, I worked at a grocery store. I made a prayer list of all my fellow employees and began to pray for them. God immediately started opening doors for me to share Jesus, and several of them became Christians!

A great example of witnessing to ones' neighbors and associates is the Apostle Levi (Matthew). As soon as he began following Jesus, he invited his neighbors and business associates to his home for a meal so they could meet his new Savior, Jesus (Luke 5:27-29). Donna and I have friends who named their son Matthew, praying he will be a person who invites those he knows to Jesus. Matthew has grown into his parents' vision and prayers; the boy has never met a stranger, and he invites them to Jesus and church!

Anyone can get to know their neighbors and associates at work, school, or other places, begin to pray for them, and then share Jesus as the Lord opens doors for that to happen. And He *will* open those doors!

Circle 6—Acquaintances. Most every day you interact with others such as bank tellers, store owners, waitresses, etc. These are people you see periodically on an ongoing basis. Write their names down and start praying for them. Ask the Lord to give you the opportunity to witness to them. It will be a fun adventure as you see God prepare the way for you to share Jesus!

Circle 7—Person "X". This category refers to the stranger you meet for the first time and you sense that God wants you to share Jesus with him or her. God will do that sometimes. Philip had never met the Ethiopian eunuch before, yet God called Philip to share Jesus with him (Acts 8:26f).

Here in Memphis, I go periodically with others from our church to Beale Street to pray for people and share Jesus with them. It always surprises me how many are open to hear our personal testimonies and listen to us share a brief Gospel presentation.

I also embraced a great method of sharing Jesus with strangers back in 2006. A staff member at our church, Phil Newberry, and I were eating lunch at a restaurant. He asked the server to tell us her name. He then said, "We're about to pray for our meal. Is there any specific way we can pray for you?" She teared up and said, "Yes, there is!" She then gladly gave us her prayer request. Later, we were able to share Jesus, even though before that day we had never met her! I've since used that simple witnessing method to share Jesus with hundreds of restaurant servers.

When the Holy Spirit prompts you to witness to someone, even if that person is a stranger, go ahead and do it. That prompting does not come from your sinful, fleshly nature. Nor is it from the devil. Every prompting to share Jesus comes from the Holy Spirit! And it is always good to obey Him.

You do not have to know someone personally to witness to him. You just need to love that person with the love of the Lord.

Praying Effectively for Lost People

How do we pray effectively for lost people? We can pray for conviction, conversion, and a contact.

Pray for conviction. Unless the Lord convicts a person and shows him, (1) he is a sinner, (2) his "righteousness" is not enough to save him, and (3) he will one day stand before God at the final judgment and give an account for all he did in his life, that person will not get saved. That is why we should pray that God will convict lost people of "sin, righteousness, and judgment" (cf. John 16:7-8). Without conviction, there will be no genuine conversion.

Pray for conversion. It is biblical to pray for lost people to be saved. Paul prayed for his Jewish brethren to be saved in Romans 10:1, "Brethren, my heart's desire and my prayer to God for them is for their salvation." If Paul prayed for lost people to be converted to Jesus, so should we.

When I pray for lost people, I like to pray Scripture. I pray Acts 3:19, "Father, I pray for _____. Help him to repent and return to You that his sins may be wiped away, in order that times and seasons of refreshing may come to him from Your presence." I also pray Romans 10:13, "Lord, I pray that _____ will call on Your name and be saved!"

When we pray, God does things He does not do if we don't pray. The more you pray for lost people and share Jesus with lost people, the more lost people will get saved!

Pray for a contact. Ask the Lord to bring someone into that lost person's path that will share Jesus with him. Then be prepared to be that person. God uses saved people to share Jesus with lost people. That's why Paul said, "But how can they call on him to save them unless they believe in him? And how can they believe in him if they have never heard about him? And how can they hear about him unless someone tells them?" (Rom. 10:14 NLT)

You will see more people become Christians if you will pray fervently for people by name to be *convicted* by the Holy Spirit, to be *converted* to Jesus, and to be *contacted* by a soul-winner.

Challenge:

Do you have a list of names of lost people? If not, use the Thompson's "concentric circles" plan to identify those people. Pray for them to be convicted, converted, and for God to send them a contact. And be willing to be that contact!

For Memory and Meditation:

"Brethren, my heart's desire and my prayer to God for them is for their salvation" (Rom. 10:1).

Chapter 8
Introduction and Personal Testimony

"Whether He is a sinner, I do not know;
one thing I do know, that though I was
blind, now I see." (John 9:25)

When a Christian shares Jesus with a lost person, how does he begin the conversation? Is there a way to share Jesus that seems natural not only for the person sharing, but also for the person listening?

Every writer and speaker knows that a good introduction is essential to effective communication. In this chapter you will learn how to naturally and politely change a secular conversation into an evangelistic conversation. You will also learn how to communicate your personal testimony, which is one of the most effective evangelistic tools any Christian has.

Introduction to Sharing Jesus

For some people, conversation in general is awkward. People who are introverted and shy often struggle to "break the ice" and start a conversation. Indeed, all of us know what it's like to be in a conversation that's uncomfortable because we don't know how to effectively initiate and/or continue the dialogue.

Anyone can improve his conversational skills, and any Christian can improve his evangelistic conversational skills. When you are traveling, it helps to have a good map to find your destination. Likewise, having a mental map of a Gospel presentation helps you arrive at the desired outcome—sharing Jesus with a lost person.

Part of my mental map in sharing Jesus is the acronym F.I.R.E. Those four letters are at the beginning of my evangelistic map. F.I.R.E. stands for: Family, Interests, Religious background, and Exploratory questions.[4] These four areas provide a helpful introduction when we share Jesus.

Family. Most people enjoy talking about themselves and their families. Thus, it is usually effective to ask the person with whom you are sharing about general information regarding their family. Some appropriate questions might be:

- "Are you married?" If so, "How did you and your spouse meet?"
- "How long have you been married?"
- "Where do you live?"
- "Do you have children?" If so, "What are their ages?"
- "Are your parents still living?" If so, "Where do they live?"
- Ask other appropriate questions.

---

[4]The acronym **F.I.R.E.** comes from the former Continued Witnessing Training (C.W.T.) materials from the North American Mission Board (N.A.M.B.) of the Southern Baptist Convention. Used here by permission.

As you engage people with these questions regarding their family, listen carefully to their responses so you'll be able to continue the conversation in a way that interests them. Keeping them interested in the conversation is essential.

As you follow the information they offer, you can branch out to better connect with them. If someone says, "We were married thirty years ago in Mississippi," I'd respond by saying, "My wife and I have been married since 1980. And I was actually born in Mississippi." Making such connections can help engage the person. Talk with people about their families!

Interests. Another effective way to connect with people is to discuss their various interests. For instance, a man might be wearing a hat or a shirt with the emblem of a sports team. If so, it's natural to say, "Are you a (name of their team) fan?" Or if someone is wearing a uniform that suggests their profession, feel free to say, "Thank you for what you do." A simple comment like that can engage someone in a conversation that opens the door for sharing Jesus.

Most people enjoy talking about sports, music, hobbies, a book they are reading, and so on. Ask them questions about those things. Read the Gospels and see how often Jesus engaged people by asking questions. Use their interests to initiate and perpetuate a conversation.

Religious Background. Talking about secular things is a great start, but how do we get to the point in the conversation where we actually share Jesus? After you have engaged a person by talking about family and various interests, one of the best ways to do this is to ask about their religious background.

Following a hypothetical conversation I mentioned above, I could help the conversation become evangelistic by saying, "I also grew up in Mississippi. We lived in Corinth, and my father worked on the railroad. We attended First Baptist Church. As a child I was impressed with the beautiful building with its extremely tall steeple."

After the person responds, then I could say, "My parents always took us to church. Now my family and I attend Bellevue Baptist Church here in Memphis. *What about you? Do you attend church?*"

This simple, straightforward approach, by which you ask polite questions about a person's religious background, will tell you a great deal about his spiritual condition. Christians who are actively involved in a church usually let you know immediately. In the same way, people who don't attend church usually tell you that as well. The moment you discover a person's religious background, the conversation changes from secular to evangelistic. At that point, it is appropriate to ask two questions.

Exploratory Questions. A medical doctor assesses a patient with exploratory questions. He might ask, "What are your symptoms? How long has this pain bothered you? Has anyone else in your family ever suffered with these symptoms?"

Just as a medical doctor uses questions to diagnose a patient, those believers sharing Jesus should make use of exploratory questions. Here are two exploratory questions you can use when you share Jesus with lost people:

Question 1: "Do you know for certain that you have eternal life and you will go to Heaven when you die, or would you say that is something you are still working on?"

This question obviously seeks to find out whether the person is certain about his salvation in Christ. The opening phrase, "Do you know for certain," is sobering. It cuts to the heart of being assured of one's salvation.

When people are genuinely saved, they'll usually let you know immediately. They'll say something like…

- "Yes, I've trusted Jesus Christ as my Savior and Lord."
- "Yes, I've known the Lord a long time. He saved me at the age of ___."

However, when you ask someone this exploratory question, and he is either not saved or not certain of his salvation, there will usually be an apparent awkwardness in his response. Some of the most common answers from lost people that I've heard over the years regarding this exploratory question are:

- "I'm not sure anyone can know that for certain."
- "I *think* I know I'll go to Heaven when I die, but I'm not 100 percent sure."

- "I hope so."
- "I guess I'm still working on that."

These types of responses are indicators that a person is probably lost.

Question 2: "If you stood before God and He asked you, 'Why should I let you into Heaven?' what would you say?" [5]

This second exploratory question seeks to determine the basis of the person's hopes of being saved. You're asking him what he believes the requirements are to enter Heaven. Some of the more frequent answers to this question I've heard by people who are not Christians are:

- "I'm not sure what I'd say to God if He asked me that."
- "I'd tell God, 'I'm a good person and try to do the best I can.'"
- "I'd say, 'I believe in You, God.'"
- "I'd say, 'I think I'm as good as anybody else.'"

What these answers imply is that they are trusting in themselves and their good works to save them and allow them into Heaven, and they are not trusting in Jesus. That is why they are lost. The Bible says that human religious works never save anyone. The Apostle Paul wrote, "[God] saved us, not on the basis of deeds which we have done in

---

[5] These two questions are modifications of the C.W.T. questions. Used by permission.

righteousness, but according to His mercy, by the washing of regeneration and renewing by the Holy Spirit" (Titus 3:5). Religious works save no one. Instead, we can only be saved by the grace of God. Salvation is a free gift. It cannot be earned, and no one deserves it.

These questions help us: (1) make a spiritual diagnosis regarding whether or not someone is assured of his salvation, and (2) understand what the person believes are the requirements for being saved and entering Heaven.

Your Personal Testimony

Another tool for effectively sharing Jesus with a lost person is sharing your personal testimony of how Jesus saved you.

The New Testament tells us about a man in the first century who was born blind. Jesus healed him by giving him sight. When people asked him how he could now see, he told them Jesus had healed him. This infuriated the Jewish religious leaders of that day because Jesus healed him on the Sabbath. When they interrogated the man about his healing, he gave a testimony that has become famous: "Whether He is a sinner, I do not know; one thing I do know, that though I was blind, now I see" (John 9:25). How could anyone argue with that?

Twice we see the Apostle Paul sharing with people how he came to receive Jesus as Lord and Savior. Paul was the greatest theologian the church has ever known. Yet in Acts 22, while speaking before a hostile Jewish crowd, he said,

"Brethren, and fathers, hear my defense which I now offer to you" (Acts 22:1). His defense was his personal testimony. Later, before King Agrippa, Paul again, "proceeded to make his defense" (Acts 26:1). How did Paul defend himself? He shared his story, his personal experience of how he came to know Jesus. If sharing one's testimony was powerful and wise enough for the theologian Paul, it is necessary and appropriate for any believer today.

God uses our personal testimonies to create a spiritual hunger in the hearts of those with whom we share Jesus. So, how do you share your personal testimony in a witnessing conversation?

Tell others what life was like before you met Jesus. Describe how you felt before knowing Jesus as Savior and Lord. Tell of your sense of purposelessness, guilt and shame caused by sin, or confusion about the meaning of life. Tell them how you struggled with sin prior to knowing Jesus in salvation. Even a child can give a testimony and tell about how the Lord caused him to feel sorry for his sins against God.

But remember, you do *not* need to share details about your former sins. Your aim is to give glory to God, not the devil. Instead, when talking about your former sins, speak in general terms. Say something like: "Before I met Jesus, I was involved in things that were wrong. If my parents had known what I was doing it would have broken their hearts." Keep it general. Don't exalt sin or the devil; exalt Jesus!

Tell others how you came to sense your need for salvation. Talk about how you moved from merely recognizing you were a sinner to the fact that you yearned for Jesus to save you. If someone shared Jesus with you to bring about that desire, describe how it happened. If you came under conviction by reading the Bible or a Gospel tract, tell them exactly how it happened. Tell them, "I began to sense my need for salvation because…"

Tell others how you were converted to Christ. Briefly describe how you were saved. Who shared Jesus with you? How did they lead you to faith in Him? What was it like when you *repented* of your sin, *believed* in Jesus and called on His name, *receiving* Him as your Savior and Lord?

Tell others what your life is like now that you are saved. Contrast what your life was like before you met Jesus to what it is like now that He has become your Savior. Say something like, "Before I met Jesus, I worried about almost everything. But now I enjoy peace that can only come from Him." Or, "Before I met Jesus I carried a load of guilt, but now I'm free!"

Again, your personal testimony can be shared anytime once the conversation goes from secular to evangelistic (see above). Your testimony is a powerful evangelistic tool. It shows that you were once lost like them, but you found salvation in Jesus. It shows them that when it comes to salvation in Jesus, you're not a salesman; you're a satisfied customer!

Challenge:

Memorize the acronym **F.I.R.E.** as your mental map to help you politely change a secular conversation into an evangelistic conversation. Then develop your personal testimony according to the suggestions mentioned above and begin sharing your story with people who need the Savior you have—Jesus!

For Memory and Meditation:

"Whether He is a sinner, I do not know; one thing I do know, that though I was blind, now I see" (John 9:25).

Chapter 9
A Gospel Presentation

"He brought him to Jesus." (John 1:42)

In the previous chapter, we analyzed the **Introduction** to our evangelistic road map. We learned how to engage a lost person in a conversation with the goal of sharing Jesus with him. That conversation should begin by asking questions about the person's **Family**. After that, we can discuss his various **Interests**. Then the Lord will open a door for us to discuss his **Religious Background.** That is when we should look for an opportunity to ask about his involvement in a church.

Once we have established the person's religious background and understand his connection with a church, the dialogue has changed from a secular conversation to an evangelistic one. We are now able to ask permission to ask two **Exploratory Questions.** These questions will help us determine: (1) if the person is saved, and (2) what he believes is necessary for someone to be saved and go to Heaven.

After the exploratory questions are asked and answered, it is time to share the Gospel. A great transition statement from the exploratory questions to the beginning of the Gospel presentation is, "If you have just a few minutes, I'd like to share with you how I came to know that I have eternal life and how you can also. Is that alright?"

If he says "No" then talk with him for a moment and ask him again. If he says "No" again, honor his decision, just as God does. The evangelistic part of the conversation is over. You can talk about something else with the hopes of discussing the Gospel with him again in the future.

On the other hand, if he says, "Yes, I'd like to hear more about that," then proceed to share Jesus using a Gospel presentation.

Presenting the Gospel

The outline of the Gospel presentation we will use in *Share Jesus Like It Matters* is given in detail in Appendix A at the end of this book. I advise you to make a copy of it and carry it with you. Keep a copy in your Bible to refer to. In time, you might even be able to memorize it. Hopefully it will be something you use the rest of your life. My mother wrote down an outline like this and used it to win many people to Christ. Let's analyze this outline (our evangelistic roadmap) and see how it can help us share Jesus.

Below, I have given a hypothetical evangelistic conversation so you can see how you can use the outline to share the Gospel. The actual outline as given in Appendix A will appear in bold print in the conversation to help you follow more easily. In the example below, I'll share Jesus with a lost man named Tom. I will pick up at the point after the two exploratory questions in the Introduction have been asked and answered.

Example: Evangelistic Conversation

"Tom, after hearing your response to my questions, if you have just a few minutes, I'd like to share with you how I came to know that I have eternal life and how you can also. Is that alright?" (Assuming Tom says "Yes," I'll proceed.)

"Tom, the Bible says that **God loves you.** He created you in His image. He knows everything about you. He says in the Bible, **'I have loved you with an everlasting love'** **(Jer. 31:3).** The Bible actually says that God loves everyone. Jesus said, **'For God so loved the world, that He gave His only begotten Son, that whoever believes in Him shall not perish, but have eternal life' (John 3:16).** According to Scripture, God loves all people, and God loves you!

"But the same Bible that says that God loves you also says **you are a sinner.** Sin is simply breaking God's laws. In fact, the Bible says, **'Sin is lawlessness' (1 John 3:4).** Every one of us is a sinner. Each of us has broken the laws of God. The Bible confirms that by saying, **'For all have sinned and fall short of the glory of God' (Rom. 3:23).**

"The Bible goes on to say that **God is holy and must punish sin.** God loves all of us, but He hates our sin, just as a parent loves his children but hates when they disobey him. God has to punish our sin because He is holy and righteous. Scripture says, **'[The LORD] will by no means leave the guilty unpunished' (Ex. 34:7).**

"Just as there is a penalty for breaking the laws of man, there is also a penalty for breaking the laws of God. The Bible says, **'The wages [just penalty] of sin is death' (Rom. 6:23).** All of us are spiritually dead in our sins. We're separated from a holy God.

"So here's the situation: God loves us and wants to have fellowship with us, but we are all sinners, and this holy God must punish our sins.

"But, I have good news for you, Tom. God has the only solution for your sin problem. He loves you too much to leave you in your state of being dead in sin and spiritually separated from Him. So **God sent His Son, Jesus, to save you.**

"Who is Jesus? Jesus is the sinless Son of God. He was born of a virgin. He was born free from a sinful nature like you and I have. The Bible also says that, '[Jesus] has been tempted in all things as we are, yet without sin' (Heb. 4:15). He was tempted in every manner to sin, but He never yielded to even one temptation. And although He was sinless, Jesus went to the cross and died as an atoning sacrifice to pay for the sins of all people ever to live.

"Jesus died for your sins, Tom. Jesus has already paid your sin debt so you don't have to. Jesus stayed on the cross until He paid for the sins of everyone so that anyone can be saved. On the cross Jesus cried out, 'It is finished!'(John 19:30). That means, 'Paid in full!' After Jesus died to pay our sin debt, He was buried to prove that He was really dead. Then three days after He died, **Jesus rose from the dead!**

"The Bible affirms both Jesus' atoning death and His bodily resurrection by saying, 'Christ died for our sins according to the Scriptures… He was buried… and He was raised on the third day according to the Scriptures (1 Cor. 15:3-4).

"Tom, Jesus died for your sins and rose from the dead because He wants to give you eternal life. He wants to save you. Jesus said, 'He who believes in the Son has eternal life; but he who does not obey the Son will not see life, but the wrath of God abides on him' (John 3:36).

"Tom, Jesus is offering you the gift of eternal life right now. The Bible says, 'Behold, now is "the acceptable time," behold, now is "the day of salvation"' (2 Cor. 6:2).

"So, what must you do to be saved? The first thing you must do is to **repent of your sin.** Jesus stressed this when He said, 'Unless you repent, you will all likewise perish' (Luke 13:3). To repent means to do a spiritual 'U-turn,' a spiritual 'about-face.' The Lord helps you turn from your sin and turn to Him for forgiveness. Repentance is a change of heart that results in a change of action. You *admit* your sin to God, and then ask Him to help you *quit* your sin! That's exactly what Peter had in mind when he said, **'Therefore repent and return, so that your sins may be wiped away, in order that times of refreshing may come from the presence of the Lord' (Acts 3:19).**

"Tom, God wants *everyone* to repent and be saved. The Bible declares this clearly by saying, **'God is now declaring to men that all people everywhere should repent' (Acts 17:30).** The fact that God commands 'all people everywhere' to repent means that anyone can repent and turn to Him for salvation. If God says you ought to do something, then He implies that you can do it. Tom, God commands all of us to repent; therefore we can and should repent and turn from our sins.

"After you repent of your sin, you must *believe* **in Jesus.** You must believe that Jesus died for your sins and that He rose from the dead to give you eternal life. The Bible says: **'Believe in the Lord Jesus, and you will be saved, you and your household' (Acts 16:31).** The Bible also says, **'If you confess with your mouth Jesus as Lord, and believe in your heart that God raised Him from the dead, you will be saved' (Rom. 10:9).**

"After you repent of your sin and believe in Jesus, you must *receive* **Jesus as Savior and Lord.** You must willingly accept Jesus into your life by yielding yourself to Him and inviting Him into your life to save you. God offers you eternal life in Jesus, but you must receive His offer. Salvation is available to all, but only those who receive Jesus will be saved. Scripture tells us, **'But as many as received Him, to them He gave the right to become children of God, even to those who believe in His name' (John 1:12).** You accept Jesus as Savior and Lord by calling on Him in prayer. The Bible confirms that by saying, **'Whoever will call upon the name of the LORD will be saved' (Rom. 10:13).**

"Tom, if this makes sense to you, is there any *good* reason why you should not receive Jesus as your Savior and Lord right now?" (If Tom answers, "Yes," then review the Gospel presentation with him. If Tom says, "No," then proceed. For the sake of brevity, we will assume Tom said, "No, there is no good reason I should not receive Jesus").

"That's wonderful, Tom. Let me take just a minute to **clarify** and **review** what I've said about the **Gospel** to make sure you understand. **Do you understand that God loves you?** (He answers, 'Yes'). **Do you understand that you are a sinner?** (He answers, 'Yes'). **Do you understand that God is holy and must punish your sin?** (He answers, 'Yes'). **Do you understand that God sent His Son, Jesus, to save you?** (He answers, 'Yes'). **Do you understand that Jesus was sinless, yet He died for your sins and rose from the dead, and He wants to give you eternal life?** (He answers, 'Yes').

"Then Tom, if you understand all of that, you are ready to receive Jesus! I'd like for us to **pray.** First, I'd like to pray **for you to understand** what you are doing. You are repenting of your sin, believing in Jesus, and receiving Him as your Savior and Lord. (You will now pray for understanding).

"Now, Tom, I'd like to **lead you in a prayer of surrender and commitment (use Gospel presentation).** Just mindlessly repeating these words will not save you, but if you are sincere about what you are saying to the Lord, He promises to save you! Pray something like this, Tom:

(Say a short phrase of this prayer at a time and allow him to pray that part of the prayer. Proceed through the entire prayer).

> *Dear God, thank you that You love me (Tom prays this phrase after you, and so forth through the rest of this prayer). I know that I am a sinner. I cannot save myself. Jesus, I believe that You are the only*

Savior. God, I have broken Your laws. I am guilty before You. I know that You are holy and that You must punish my sin. Thank You for sending Your Son, Jesus, to save me. Lord, I repent of my sin. By the help of Your Spirit, I turn from my sin and I turn to You. I believe that Jesus died as an atoning sacrifice for my sins and rose bodily from the dead to give me eternal life. Lord Jesus, I receive You as my Savior and Lord. I call on Your name—save me right now, Lord Jesus! Wash me and cleanse me from my sins. Fill me with Your Spirit. Help me to live for You for the rest of my life. And when I die, take me to Heaven. In Jesus' name, amen!

After Tom prays to receive Christ, **offer a prayer of thanksgiving.** After that prayer, share some appropriate verses of Scripture with him, such as John 6:47 and John 10:28, that will give him **assurance** of salvation.

You should also engage in **follow-up. Set a follow-up meeting** in the next week. Encourage and instruct Tom to begin to **read** the **Bible, pray, fellowship** with other believers, and tell someone else about his conversion. Even as a new Christian, Tom needs to learn to **share Jesus.**

Then join the angels and rejoice that someone who was lost has been saved!

Challenge:

Review the Gospel outline in Appendix A. Make a copy of it, and carry it with you so you can use it to share Jesus with lost people. Seek to memorize the Gospel outline, including the scriptures, so you can extemporaneously share Jesus with people wherever you are.

For Memory and Meditation:

"He brought him to Jesus." (John 1:42)

Chapter 10
The Sinner's Prayer: Asking Jesus into Your Heart

"If you confess with your mouth Jesus
as Lord, and believe in your heart that
God raised Him from the dead, you will
be saved; for with the heart a person
believes, resulting in righteousness, and
with the mouth he confesses, resulting
in salvation. For 'Whoever will call upon
the name of the Lord will be saved."
(Rom. 10:9-10, 13)

This book, *Share Jesus Like It Matters*, utilizes the biblical means of praying a "sinner's prayer" to help a lost person express himself to God as he repents of his sin, believes in Jesus, and receives Jesus as Savior and Lord. According to our text, and others like it, the Bible validates the appropriateness of praying and confessing with your *mouth* and calling on the name of the Lord Jesus from your *heart* for salvation.

When a lost sinner calls on Jesus through a prayer of repentance and faith, God sends His Holy Spirit to dwell eternally in that person's heart. The indwelling Spirit is actually Christ living in that person (Gal. 4:6). God adopts him, and the Spirit of His Son, Jesus, indwells his heart, causing him to cry out, "Abba, Father!"

Because God commands all people everywhere to repent (Acts 17:30), desires for all people everywhere to be saved (1 Tim. 2:3-4), and does not desire for anyone to perish (2 Pet. 3:9), anyone can be saved. Because Jesus died for the sins of everyone in the whole world (1 John 2:2), His atoning sacrifice causes all people to be savable.

When we analyze Romans 10:9-10, 13, we see that when someone prays and confesses with his mouth and believes with his heart, it is synonymous with, "asking Jesus into your heart." Yet some Christians complain that the phrases, "asking Jesus into your heart" or "inviting Christ into your life," are not found in Scripture. According to them, we should not utilize these phrases when we share Jesus.

This is merely a "straw man" argument. While it is true that these exact phrases do not appear in the New Testament, the truths do appear. That's also the case for phrases such as "biblical inerrancy" and "the Trinity." While those exact words are not in the Bible, the truths are in the Bible.

Theologian Wayne Grudem validates the use of a sinner's prayer.[6] Veteran pastors such as Charles Spurgeon[7] and John MacArthur[8] have also utilized a sinner's prayer at the end of their sermons to help non-Christians trust savingly in Christ.

---

[6] Wayne Grudem, *Systematic Theology: An Introduction to Biblical Doctrine* (Grand Rapids, Michigan: Zondervan, 1994), 717.

[7] Charles H. Spurgeon, "A Free Grace Promise," in vol. 35 of *Spurgeon's Sermons,* electronic ed. (Albany, Oregon: Ages Software, 1998).

[8] John MacArthur, "Looking at the Cross from God's Perspective" (sermon, Grace Community Church, Sun Valley, California, August 4, 1991), http://www.gty.org/resources/sermons/80-83/looking-at-the-cross-from-gods-perspective (accessed March 18, 2013).

Some object that many have prayed such a prayer, but in time, their lack of perseverance indicates that obviously they were not genuinely converted to Christ. Without question, someone can pray a sinner's prayer and either not understand what is at stake or not be sincere. If that happens, praying a sinner's prayer will not be a means to salvation for that person. Mindlessly mouthing the words of a sinner's prayer is *not* a magical method of attaining salvation.

But what goes for the sinner's prayer goes for all prayer. When we say words in "prayer," but do not mean them, any such prayer is not heard by God. However, the fact that some are insincere when they pray does not negate the fact that the Bible clearly states that in order to be saved, you must call on the name of the Lord. Calling on the Lord is prayer.

Many who pray to receive Christ at an early age actually experience legitimate conversion. But because they do not experience sufficient follow-up and discipleship, they are hindered in their spiritual growth. Nevertheless, poor discipleship practices do *not* indicate that calling on the name of the Lord via a sinner's prayer is invalid or unscriptural.

Even when the Bible simply tells us to "believe," and we do so, that kind of believing involves a prayer in the sense that there must be a turning to God, a yielding of oneself to God, a surrendering of the will toward Him. While prayer does not have to be verbalized, we must respond to God by calling out to Him in repentant, faith-filled prayer in order to be saved. You can mindlessly and meaninglessly pray a sinner's prayer and not get saved, but you cannot get saved without responding to God in prayer, calling on Jesus!

Let's focus on three issues:

God Desires to Transform Our Sinful Hearts

In the Old Testament, God predicted He would change the hearts of repentant, faith-filled men. The New Covenant would be superior to the Old Covenant. The Law promised that after Israel would break the commandments and be cursed, God would circumcise their hearts. Deuteronomy 30:6 says, "The LORD your God will circumcise your heart and the heart of your descendants, to love the LORD your God with all your heart and with all your soul, so that you may live."

Jeremiah built on this as the basis for the New Covenant. Stressing the relationship between the Law and the human heart, he wrote, "Circumcise yourselves to the LORD and remove the foreskins of your heart" (Jer. 4:4). He also said, "But this is the covenant which I will make with the house of Israel after those days," declares the Lord, "I will put My law within them and on their heart I will write it; and I will be their God, and they shall be my people" (Jer. 31:33).

Ezekiel also promised a future heart-work performed by God for His people. The Spirit Himself would indwell them. He said in Ezekiel 36:26-27, "I will give you a new heart and put a new spirit within you; and I will remove the heart of stone from your flesh and give you a heart of flesh. I will put my Spirit within you and cause you to walk in My statutes, and you will be careful to obey My ordinances."

The New Testament writers continued to expand on this concept. Paul said in Romans 2:28-29, "For he is not a Jew who is one outwardly, nor is circumcision that which is outward in the flesh. But he is a Jew who is one inwardly; and circumcision is that which is of the heart, by the Spirit, not by the letter; and his praise is not from men, but from God."

Paul also affirmed that Christ resides in the hearts of Christians. He said in Colossians 3:15, "Let the peace of Christ rule in your hearts..." Likewise, Peter admonished in 1 Peter 3:15, "But sanctify Christ as Lord in your hearts."

In the Old Testament, God promised to do something new by transforming the hearts of men and women who repented of their sin and placed their faith in God's Messiah. In the New Testament, God fulfilled that promise.

God Desires to Indwell Individuals with His Holy Spirit

The indwelling Spirit within a believer is a major New Testament theme. Jesus said, "The Spirit of truth, whom the world cannot receive, because it does not see Him or know Him, but you know Him because He abides with you and will be in you" (John 14:17). Paul also said, "However, you are not in the flesh but in the Spirit, if indeed the Spirit of God dwells in you. But if anyone does not have the Spirit of Christ, he does not belong to Him" (Rom. 8:9).

When the Holy Spirit came upon Mary, she was overshadowed with the power of the Most High God. Jesus literally, physically came into her body (Luke 1:31f). Today, whenever a person is saved, the Spirit also "comes upon" that person spiritually (Acts 1:8), baptizes that person into Christ, and causes that person to partake and drink of the Holy Spirit (1 Cor. 12:13). Just as Christ was birthed physically in Mary's womb when the Holy Spirit came upon her, even so He is birthed spiritually in the heart of every believer whenever the Holy Spirit comes upon him at conversion.

No wonder Paul could say in Colossians 1:27, "Christ in you [is] the hope of glory," and in Ephesians 3:16-17, "That He would grant you, according to the riches of His glory, to be strengthened with power through His Spirit in the inner man, so that Christ may dwell in your hearts through faith."

God desires to indwell individuals with His Holy Spirit.

God Desires for People to Be Saved

What must transpire for a person to be saved?

We must be exposed to the Gospel. Romans 10:13-14 says, "For 'Whoever will call upon the name of the Lord will be saved.' How then will they call on Him in whom they have not believed? How will they believe in Him whom they have not heard? And how will they hear without a preacher?"

No one can be saved until he has access to the Gospel of Jesus. Ephesians 1:13 says, "In Him, you also, after listening to the message of truth, the gospel of your salvation—having also believed, you were sealed in Him with the Holy Spirit of promise." Here we see the biblical *Ordo Salutis*, "the order of salvation," where: (1) we hear the truth of the Gospel, (2) we believe, and (3) we are sealed in and saved by Jesus through the Holy Spirit.

We must *repent* of sin. Jesus said, "Unless you repent, you will all likewise perish" (Luke 13:3). Paul told his listeners, "Therefore repent and return, so that your sins may be wiped away, in order that times of refreshing may come from the presence of the Lord; and that He may send Jesus, the Christ appointed for you" (Acts 3:19-20). To repent is to do a spiritual "U-turn." One turns away from his wicked ways and then turns to God.

We must *believe* in Jesus. In His first sermon, Jesus said, "Repent and believe in the gospel" (Mark 1:15). We must believe in our hearts that Jesus died for our sins and rose from the dead. We must place our faith and trust in what Jesus has done to secure our salvation. We are saved by and justified through faith in Jesus (Eph. 2:8; Rom. 5:1).

We must *receive* Jesus as Lord and Savior. The Bible says, "But as many as received Him, to them He gave the right to become children of God, even to those who believe in His name" (John 1:12). The word "receive" is the Greek word *lambano*, which means, "to accept as true, receive, take hold of, seize, choose, select." The concept of "receiving and accepting Jesus" is found throughout John's writings (John 7:39; 12:48; 13:20; 14:17; 20:22).

We must *call* on Jesus' name in prayer. Calling on the name of the Lord is prayer, and any sinner can pray for salvation.

Soon after Cain murdered his brother Abel, we read, "Then men began to call upon the name of the Lord" (Gen. 4:26). That obviously refers to prayer. Others like Abraham (Gen. 12:8), Moses (Ex. 34:5), David (1 Chron. 16:8), Elijah (1 Kings 18:24), Isaiah (Isa. 55:6-7), Hosea (Hos. 14:1-2), Joel (Joel 2:32), Peter (Acts 2:21), Paul (Rom. 10:13), Ananias (Acts 22:16), either called on God in prayer, or encouraged others to do so.

What is "praying a sinner's prayer" for salvation if it is not calling on the name of the Lord?

While we all agree that no exact wording of a sinner's prayer is prescribed in Scripture, and there is no "official" sinner's prayer, yet a heartfelt prayer by a lost sinner is still a valid, scriptural truth that assists people as they call on Jesus' name and *respond* to the Gospel!

The thief on the cross (Luke 23:42), the former blind man (John 9:35-38), and the repentant tax collector (Luke 18:13), didn't all pray the same words, but they all believed in their hearts and confessed Jesus with their mouths. Consequently, they were all saved!

When a sinner repents, believes, and receives Jesus, calling on His name in prayer for salvation, Jesus regenerates that person and comes to dwell in his heart through the Holy Spirit. With that understanding, the phrase "asking Jesus into your heart" is indeed a biblical truth.

In fact, the phrase "invite Jesus into your heart," just might be one of the best ways to articulate the fundamental difference between the Old and New Covenants.

Challenge:

Have you *repented* of your sin, *believed* in and *received* Jesus, calling on His name through a sinner's prayer to ask Him to live in your heart through His indwelling Holy Spirit? If not, do that today.

Ask those in your class to share when they prayed and asked Jesus into their hearts as well. Make sure everyone in your class has been saved.

For Memory and Meditation:

"Whoever will call upon the name of the LORD will be saved" (Rom. 10:13).

Chapter 11
Now That You're Saved

"But grow in the grace and knowledge
of our Lord and Savior Jesus Christ. To
Him be the glory, both now and to the
day of eternity. Amen." (2 Pet. 3:18)

Once a person is saved, he needs to mature and grow in
Christlikeness. This chapter is designed to help a new believer
in Jesus do just that. It does not set forth a comprehensive
treatment of Christian discipleship. Rather, it offers helpful
information that will assist a new Christian in getting a good
start in the Christian life. Let's look at some of the most
common questions new Christians ask, and answer them
biblically.

Biblical Answers to Common Questions

Can I Know That I'm Saved?
This question has already been dealt with thoroughly in
Chapter 6. Suffice it to say that the Bible clearly states we
can be assured of our salvation in Jesus. We read in 1 John
5:13, "These things I have written to you who believe in the
name of the Son of God, so that you may know that you have
eternal life." "Know" means that we can be absolutely certain

we are saved. We don't have a "hope-so salvation," we have a "know-so salvation"!

The Bible says, "Test yourselves to see if you are in the faith" (2 Cor. 13:5). Here are some biblical tests for salvation:

- Have you repented of sin, believed in Jesus, and received Him? (John 1:12; Rom. 10:13)
- Do you love other Christians? (1 John 3:14)
- Do you sense the presence of the Holy Spirit? (Rom. 8:16)
- Do you desire to obey God? (1 John 2:3)
- Do you desire to read your Bible? (1 Pet. 2:2-3)
- Do you experience answered prayers? (1 John 5:14-15)

If you can honestly answer "Yes to these questions, your conversion is valid. And remember, you can never lose your salvation because no one can snatch you from God's hand (John 10:27-29), nothing can separate you from God's love (Rom. 8:38-39), and nothing can sever the seal of God's Spirit (Eph. 1:13-14).

If you have asked Jesus to save you, He has done so.

Is Baptism Important?

Jesus commands all new Christians to be baptized. He said, "Go therefore and make disciples of all the nations, *baptizing them* in the name of the Father and the Son and the Holy Spirit" (Matt. 28:19).

The New Testament teaches that baptism is exclusively for those who have already believed in Jesus (Acts 2:41). Infant baptism is not a biblical doctrine. Baptism is by immersion only (Acts 8:38-39). Neither sprinkling nor pouring ever replaces immersion as the biblical mode of baptism. According to Jesus, baptism is to be done in the name of the triune God—Father, Son, and Holy Spirit (Matt. 28:19-20). Finally, baptism does not confer salvation. Rather, it is a symbol of one's salvation (Rom. 6:4).

The biblical way for a new Christian to "go public" (i.e. confess Christ) is to be baptized.

Is Church Membership Necessary?

Church membership is biblical. The early believers engaged in official church membership. We know that partly because when a church member sinned and was unrepentant, the local church had the ability to excommunicate that person from church membership (1 Cor. 5).

Jesus founded the church. The church is called Jesus' building, and He is its very "cornerstone" (Eph. 2:20-21). Jesus is the foundation of the church (1 Cor. 3:11), the rock upon which it is built (Matt. 16:18). The church is also Jesus' *body* (Eph. 5:23). Christ is the head of the church (Col. 1:18), and Christians are the members of His body (Eph. 5:29-30). We function in harmony under His leadership. Likewise, the church is likened to Jesus' *bride* (Eph. 5:26-27). Jesus is "married" to all Christians by means of salvation. He loves us as a faithful bridegroom (Mark 2:19-20).

The Greek word for "church" is *ecclesia* meaning, "called out." Christians have been called out, set apart, and sanctified from this world to be Christ's holy people (1 Pet. 1:14-16; 2:9). We are in this world, but not of it (John 15:19). Every believer is set apart from the world to be an active member of a local church. If you love Jesus, the head of the church, you should also love other Christians who are the body of the church. If you love the foundation of the church (Jesus), you should also love the building (other Christians). If you love the groom of the church (Jesus), you should also love His bride (the church). The church at its worst is better than the world at its best.

How Can I Understand the Bible?
The Bible is God's inspired Word (2 Tim. 3:16). It not only contains truth, it is truth (John 17:17). The Bible teaches the "verbal plenary" inspiration of the Bible. "Verbal" means that the *words* of Scripture are inspired and God-breathed. "Plenary" means that *all* the words of the Bible are inspired. Every word of the Old and New Testaments is the inspired, inerrant, infallible, authoritative Word of God.

How can a Christian get to know his Bible?
Here are seven ways you can come to know your Bible:

- **Read the Bible**. Read the Scriptures systematically. Go through entire books of the Bible from beginning to end. Read slowly and out loud for better comprehension and concentration.

- **Study the Bible**. Research cross-references in the margins of your Bible. Purchase a good theologically conservative study Bible and also Bible commentaries. Join a weekly Bible study with a mature believer teaching God's Word.

- **Hear the Bible preached and taught.** Join a church that has a pastor who preaches and teaches the Bible verse-by-verse. Take notes and study them after the sermon is delivered. Hearing God's Word taught and preached will build your faith (Rom. 10:17).

- **Memorize the Bible.** Write down a verse of Scripture on a blank business card and commit it to memory. Carry memory cards with you each day, and review them regularly. Soon they will be yours for life.

- **Sing the Bible.** Sing "Scripture songs." This method has helped children memorize Scripture for years. It works for adults as well. Also, listen to music that is based on God's Word.

- **Display the Bible.** Display paintings and pictures in your home and office with Scripture verses written on them. Place such pictures in every room as a powerful, silent reminder of the truth of God's Word.

- **Meditate on the Bible.** Meditate on the Scriptures. Mull over God's Word again and again as you ask the Holy Spirit to guide you into all truth (John 16:13).

How Do I Pray?

Prayer is intimate communication with God. It is a conversation, a dialogue, not a monologue. How can we learn to pray?

- **Listen to God.** God speaks to His children primarily through the Bible. The more time we spend in the Bible, the more we will think God's thoughts. God also speaks to Christians through the promptings of the indwelling Holy Spirit. He speaks and guides us in decision-making and in service to others. We should remain in a constant state of prayer, walking in the Spirit (Gal. 5:16, 25), listening to the gentle whisper of His voice.

- **Talk to God.** God wants us to come to Him as a child coming to a loving Father. Several types of prayers are mentioned in Scripture:

   Prayer of Adoration—Praise God for who He is.

   Prayer of Thanksgiving—Thank God for what He has done.

   Prayer of Confession—Confess and repent of your sins.

   Prayer of Intercession—Pray and intercede for the needs of others.

   Prayer of Petition—Pray for your own needs to be met.

   Prayer of Protection—Ask God to help you avoid or withstand temptations that come your way.

Learn to pray by spending time with a Christian who knows how to pray. Praying is as essential to the Christian's spiritual life as breathing is to one's physical life. A day without prayer is a wasted day.

Why Do I Need Christian Friends?

Once you become a Christian, your best friends should be other believers. From now on, the primary reason you should have friendships with non-Christians is to share Jesus with them. Non-evangelistic friendships with lost people can hinder a Christian spiritually. The Apostle Paul said, "Do not be deceived: 'Bad company corrupts good morals'" (1 Cor. 15:33).

Believers in Jesus must not neglect assembling together with other Christians. Fellowship encourages and stimulates us to obey Jesus and be better disciples (Heb. 10:24-25). Jesus also promised to be present with us when we gather in His name with other believers (Matt. 18:20).

How Can I Share My Faith with Others?

Immediately after a new believer is saved, he should start sharing Jesus with non-Christians.

- **Make a list of non-Christians.** Write down the names of lost people you know.
- **Begin to pray for them.** Pray for their *conviction*, for their *conversion*, and for a *contact* to share Jesus with them.

- **Share the Gospel.** Seek to share Jesus verbally with lost people for the purpose of leading them to faith in Him.
- **Give them assurance.** Once they are saved, assure them that if they repented of their sin, believed on Jesus, and called on His name, they are eternally saved!

Sharing one's faith is a privilege and also a tremendous responsibility. For more detailed information, review chapter 7.

How Do I Worship God?

Worship means "to ascribe worth-ship." God is "worthy" of our praise! As Christians, we are to love God with all our heart, soul, mind, and strength (Mark 12:30). Our worship shows our love for Him.

One way to worship is to sing praises to God. The Book of Psalms is a collection of worship songs in which we are told to sing to the Lord, extol His name, clap our hands in praise, lift our hands in His honor, play musical instruments to bless Him, and so forth. In the New Testament, additional elements of worship such as preaching biblical sermons, partaking of the Lord's Supper, baptizing new believers, collecting financial offerings, and praying are also mentioned.

Biblical worship attracts God's manifest presence (John 4:23-24) and lifts the believer to new heights of spiritual growth and maturity. It also prepares him for eternity in Heaven.

Can I Serve the Lord?

Christians serve God by serving others. When we feed the hungry, clothe the naked, and visit those who are sick or in prison, Jesus said it is as though we are doing it to Him (Matt. 25:31-45). Selfless service to others is never a burden. Rather, we are to "serve the Lord with gladness" (Ps. 100:2).

God has gifted every believer with at least one spiritual gift that will enable him to minister effectively to others. Those spiritual gifts, listed in Romans 12:6-8; 1 Corinthians 12:8-10; and Ephesians 4:11, create desires, passions, and the abilities necessary for serving the Lord in particular ways. Every Christian is vital to the body of Christ. We must avoid selfishness and think of others, putting their needs ahead of ours (Phil. 2:3-4). The Lord can then use us to minister to other people by serving them.

What Does the Bible Say about Money?

Every Christian should submit his material possessions to God and seek to honor Him financially (Prov. 3:9).

- **Practice "storehouse tithing."** In the Old Testament God's people were commanded to bring "the whole tithe" (10 percent of their earnings) to the temple storehouse, giving it in an undesignated fashion to the Lord's work (Mal. 3:10). Jesus also affirmed tithing (Matt. 23:23). Thus, Christians should tithe (give 10 percent of their earnings) to their "storehouse" which is their local church. They should give in a cheerful manner (2 Cor. 9:7), knowing that God will use their finances to spread the Gospel of Jesus at home and around the world.

- **Work to earn money.** If you are healthy and able, God expects you to work to earn a living. If a person is able to work but is simply too lazy to do so, the Bible says he should not be allowed to eat (2 Thess. 3:10). If you are physically unable to work, you deserve financial assistance. If you are healthy, get a job and go to work.

- **Live within your means.** Christians should not overspend. To do so is a poor witness. Establish a financial budget, and pay your bills on time. Avoid debt whenever possible. Save money to pay for future needs such as college, weddings, Christmas, vacations, and retirement. (cf. Prov. 6:6-11).

- **Be grateful for what God has given to you.** Thank God for the material blessings He has given you. Learn to be content with what you already have (Phil. 4:11; 1 Tim. 6:8; Heb. 13:5). Acknowledge that every good and perfect gift comes from the Lord above (James 1:17).

- **Be a blessing to others through giving.** Once you have tithed to your church and paid your bills, then it is time to give financially to others in need as the Lord prompts you. God blesses you to be a blessing to others. When possible, do so anonymously so Jesus will receive all the glory (Matt. 6:3-4).

Challenge:

If you are a new Christian, study this chapter carefully and apply it. If you have shared Jesus with someone and they have received Jesus as Savior, review the content of this chapter with them to help them get started in their new life in Jesus.

For Memory and Meditation:

"But grow in the grace and knowledge of our Lord and Savior Jesus Christ. To Him be the glory, both now and to the day of eternity. Amen" (2 Pet. 3:18).

Chapter 12
What Happens When You Die?

"For what will it profit a man if he gains
the whole world and forfeits his soul?
Or what will a man give in exchange for
his soul?" (Matt. 16:26)

"And inasmuch as it is appointed for men to die once and
after this comes judgment." (Heb. 9:27)

If Jesus delays His return, you and I will die. What then?
Do we cease to exist? Do we "recycle" spiritually and come
back in another life? Or do we stand in judgment and give an
account for our earthly lives and then face eternal Heaven or
Hell?

Bible-believing Christians adhere to the latter. We believe
that when a person dies, there is a continuation of life for
that person's soul and spirit. In fact, at Jesus' return, Christians
believe that their bodies will be resurrected from their graves
and transformed into new celestial bodies, similar to Jesus'
body after He rose from the dead. Every Christian's resurrected body will be instantaneously reunited with his spirit
and soul which are already with Jesus, and thus, we shall
forever be with the Lord (1 Thess. 4:13-18).

Biblical Christians do not believe in unbiblical doctrines
such as purgatory or reincarnation. We believe that when a

person leaves the body (i.e., when he dies) he goes to either Heaven or Hell forever.

That is why sharing Jesus is so very important. People are en route to eternity. For those who know Jesus, it will be glorious. For those who do not know Jesus, it will be horrific.

According to Jesus Christ, what happens when we die? In Luke 16:19-31, Jesus told about two men who died. Most scholars agree this was not a parable; Jesus was talking about real people. One man (his name was not given) was rich; the other man, Lazarus, was poor. When the poor man died, angels carried him to Abraham's bosom (i.e., Paradise/Heaven). When the rich man died, he was buried. The angels did not carry him away. Instead, he went to Hades where he experienced great suffering and torment. He could see Lazarus far away, resting at Abraham's right hand. He even begged Abraham to have Lazarus bring him some water to relieve his suffering. But Abraham refused, insisting that God allowed no crossing from Heaven to Hell or vice versa.

The rich man then desperately begged Abraham to send Lazarus to his five brothers to warn them about Hell. Again Abraham refused, saying that his family had the Old Testament scriptures to warn them. The rich man protested, saying that if someone rose from the dead and spoke to his family, then they would believe. Abraham corrected him by insisting that if his brothers would not listen to the Old Testament scriptures, neither would they listen to someone who rose from the dead, even if that someone was Jesus, the Messiah.

Luke 16 shows us the three primary things that will happen to you when you die.

1. Your Soul Will Leave Your Body.

When I was a young preacher, I remember going to a funeral home to visit the family of a church member who had died. The funeral home was a short distance from our church building, so I decided to walk. As I approached the funeral home, I noticed a man in a fetal position on his knees with his face down on the ground. He was dead! He apparently had just died a few seconds before I walked up to him. Furthermore, as I looked at him I recognized that he was one of the painters that had been painting all that day at our church building. We had actually said hello to one another earlier that morning. But now, just a few hours later, he was dead. His body was present, but he was gone. I could not help but wonder if his spirit and soul were in Heaven or Hell. It was obvious that something about him was missing. What was missing was his soul and spirit.

The moment you die, your soul and spirit leave your body. Your body ceases to function, but your spirit and soul don't. They live on even after your physical body is buried. Thus, death is simply the separation of your soul and spirit from your physical body.

The Bible teaches that each human is a trichotomy. We each have three essential parts—spirit, soul, and body. Paul affirmed this by writing, "Now may the God of peace Himself sanctify you entirely; and may your spirit and soul and body be preserved complete, without blame at the coming of our Lord Jesus Christ" (1 Thess. 5:23). Again, when you die, your spiritual nature (your soul and spirit) leaves your physical body.

The Bible gives several examples of this reality. For instance, when Rachel, Jacob's wife, was about to die, "it came about as her soul was departing (for she died)" (Gen. 35:18). Rachel passed away as she gave birth to her son Benjamin. Her soul departed from her body.

Jesus also spoke of another rich man who was very foolish. The more he prospered financially, the more he contemplated how he could indulge himself with his expanded riches. He did not realize that he had an imminent appointment with death. God said to Him, "Fool! This very night your soul will be required of you" (Luke 12:20). These are sobering words. At death, God requires your soul from you! God says in Ezekiel 18:4, "Behold, all souls are Mine; the soul of the father as well as the soul of the son is Mine." Your soul does not belong to you; it belongs to God! When He created you, He created you as a living soul. At conception, God put life in you. Before you could breathe earth's air, God breathed into your nostrils "the breath of life" and created you as a living soul (Gen. 2:7). You are not a body with a soul. You are a spirit and soul with a body. The body you have will waste away, but your spirit and soul will live forever. Regardless of what the atheists teach, all people are spiritual beings who possess an eternal soul. When your spirit and soul leave your body, you die.

The Bible also tells us about Stephen, the first Christian martyr, who was stoned to death. Just before he died, he prayed, "Lord Jesus, receive my spirit" (Acts 7:59). As those rocks from the angry mob slowly crushed Stephen, his spirit and soul left his body and he died.

Again, when you see a dead person, it is obvious that something is missing. That is because that person's soul and spirit have departed from his body to go to either Heaven or Hell. That is the first thing that happens when you die.

2. You Will Stand Before God in Judgment

Luke 16 shows that when a person dies, he is very much aware of his surroundings and what is happening to him in either Heaven or Hell. There is no such thing as "soul sleep." Nor does Scripture teach the false doctrine of reincarnation, where people recycle spiritually until they attain a level of eternal bliss. Rather, the Bible teaches in Hebrews 9:27, "It is appointed for men to die once and after this comes judgment." Should Jesus tarry, every person has an appointment with death. That is when you will face judgment before God. Incidentally, everyone who dies knows for certain there is a God. Rest assured, there are no atheists in eternity!

Yet, for Christians, standing before God in judgment has nothing to do with where we will spend eternity. Our destiny was decided the moment we accepted Jesus as our Lord and Savior. We will spend eternity in Heaven. Rather, judgment for Christians involves the judgment of our works that we've done on earth after we received Jesus as our Savior. The Bible says in 2 Corinthians 5:10, "For we must all appear before the judgment seat of Christ, so that each one may be recompensed for his deeds in the body, according to what he has done, whether good or bad." When a Christian dies, he immediately stands before God. Whatever he did in life that was done for any other reason than for the glory of God will be "wood, hay," or "straw" that will burn up and be gone forever. But all that he did for God's glory will be "gold, silver," and "precious stones"—treasure for him to enjoy for eternity in Heaven (1 Cor. 3:11-15).

On the other hand, a horrifying judgment awaits non-Christians. Revelation 20:11-15 gives a graphic description. If you don't know Jesus, you will stand before God at the Great White Throne of judgment. The "books" that contain the record of all your activities on earth will then be opened and reviewed. After that condemning evidence is set forth, the book of life will be opened. Since only Christians' names are in that book, all others will be cast into Hell, the lake of fire (Rev. 20:15).

3. You Will Spend Eternity Either in Heaven or Hell

The third thing that happens when you die is that you will spend eternity in either Heaven or Hell. In Luke 16, Lazarus died and was carried away by the angels to Paradise, referred to in that text as "Abraham's bosom." The rich man died and went to Hades where he was in torment. This is not the unbiblical doctrine of purgatory, teaching that some Christians go to a place of temporary torment to have their sins "purged" before they enter Heaven. Such a teaching is completely unfounded in Scripture. It is a man-made, fabricated lie. No one has his sins "purged" in purgatory before going to Heaven, nor does anyone get a second chance after death via reincarnation. Jesus said in Matthew 25:46, "These will go away into eternal punishment," (i.e., Hell), "but the righteous into eternal life" (i.e., Heaven). Here, Jesus talked about Heaven and Hell (in that order), referring to them as the only eternal destinations that await anyone after death.

If you are a Christian, you will enter Paradise when you die. Jesus told the repentant thief on the cross, "Today you shall be with Me in Paradise" (Luke 23:43). That is, immediately after he died, he went with Jesus to Heaven! Paradise is also what Jesus described in Luke 16:22 as "Abraham's bosom." It was the place where the angels carried Lazarus after he died. He was resting in Abraham's bosom (a place of prominence) in Paradise. The Apostle Paul concurs with this by saying that when a Christian is absent from his physical body, he is immediately present with the Lord (2 Cor. 5:8). That is, his spirit and soul are in Heaven. At the end of time when Jesus returns, every Christian who has been in Paradise will enter into Heaven, the celestial city called new Jerusalem, which is described vividly in Revelation 21–22.

Non-Christians go to Hades at death. At Christ's return, they will be sentenced by God at the judgment at the Great White Throne (Rev. 20:11) and be cast into Hell, the lake of fire. Dr. Herschel Hobbs used to say that Hades is like the county jail, and Hell is like the penitentiary. The "lake of fire" is Hell. The word for "Hell" in Greek is, *Gehenna*. It is derived from the "valley of *Hinnom*" in Jerusalem, which was the garbage dump outside of that city in Jesus' day. It was a wretched place with worms, fire, and stench. By referring to Hell as Gehenna, Jesus was saying, "Hell is the garbage dump of the universe." In Hell, the worm never dies, and the fire never goes out. We read in Revelation 20:14, "Then death and Hades were thrown into the lake of fire." Again, everyone who goes to Hades will go to Hell (Gehenna) after the final judgment (Rev. 21:8f).

In summary, at death, Christians go to Paradise and lost people go to Hades. At the coming of Christ, the lost people in Hades are cast into Hell, the lake of fire. The Christians who have been in Paradise will enter into the new Jerusalem.

Challenge:

All people are going to die. Each person's spirit and soul will leave his body. He will then stand before God and face judgment. He will spend eternity in either Heaven or Hell based on what he did with Jesus during his time on earth. Doesn't that motivate you all the more to share Jesus with lost people?

For Memory and Meditation:

"For what will it profit a man if he gains the whole world and forfeits his soul? Or what will a man give in exchange for his soul?" (Matt. 16:26)

"And inasmuch as it is appointed for men to die once and after this comes judgment." (Heb. 9:27)

Conclusion

All people will spend eternity in either Heaven or Hell based on what they do with Jesus during this short span of life on earth. When you think about that fact, you begin to realize how important it is for every Christian to become a soul-winner. We must constantly share Jesus with lost people in order to win them to Him.

Growing up in West Tennessee in a Baptist church, I remember the congregational singing, especially the songs about evangelism and soul-winning. I remember as a child standing between my parents at church singing, "Rescue the Perishing," "Lord, Lay Some Soul Upon My Heart," "Bringing in the Sheaves," and "I Love to Tell the Story." Those songs spoke about the urgency of sharing Jesus with lost people. I also remember our choir singing songs like Lanny Wolfe's, "My House Is Full, (But My Fields Are Empty)." That song empha-sized the sad fact that most of God's children prefer the blessings of worshiping God together in the church, rather than going outside the walls of the church building to share Jesus with lost people.

Later, as a teenager, I remember the sermons and songs of the nationwide youth revival known as the Jesus Move-ment that occurred in America in the late 1960s and early 1970s. There was a strong emphasis on personal evangelism in those days. The mantra, "One Way!" (adapted from Jesus' words in John 14:6 regarding Him being the only way to

Heaven) was heard everywhere in America. Christians were expected to share Jesus verbally with the lost. It was not uncommon to go to a mall or park and see teenagers and college students passing out Gospel tracts, sharing the Gospel with anyone who would listen.

Then when I became a young preacher in 1977, at virtually every denominational gathering I attended, someone was speaking about "soul-winning." I can remember my predecessor at Bellevue, Dr. Adrian Rogers, talking about specific lost people with whom he had recently shared Jesus.

In that day, soul-winning was the goal for every committed Christian. Evangelism was at the forefront of the church's mission. The Southern Baptist Convention experienced record conversions and baptisms during that era. Even those who did not practice evangelism at least acknowledged its importance.

But alas, soul-winning, for the most part, is now absent among American Christians. Thus, it is not surprising that at the time of this writing, Southern Baptists are experiencing some of the lowest numbers of people being saved and baptized in our denomination's history. Rarely does anyone talk about "soul-winning." Some talk about having "Gospel conversations." Yet, all too often, such "Gospel conversations" consist of more "conversation" than "Gospel."

Soul-winning involves opening our mouths and telling people what the Bible says about Jesus (Acts 8:35). That is the strategy set forth in this book. We need intentional evangelism.

My good friend and fellow pastor, Dr. James Merritt, is fond of asking two probing questions that convict me every time I hear them: (1) "When is the last time you led someone to Jesus?" and (2) "When is the last time you tried?"

Dr. Merritt insists, and I concur, that the second of those two questions is the most important. When's the last time you tried to lead someone to faith in Jesus Christ? That is, when is the last time you shared Jesus like it matters?

Sharing Jesus does matter. People are on their way to Hell. Some will go to Hell who would have gone to Heaven if we had simply shared Jesus with them. They will not go to Hell and suffer eternally because God predestined and wanted them to go to Hell. Rather, they will go to Hell largely because we did not pray for them to be saved, and because we never gave them a clear, polite, scriptural, Gospel presentation. At the final judgment, their blood will be on our hands (cf. Eze. 3:17-18; Acts 18:6; 20:26).

The great London Baptist preacher of the 1800s, Charles Spurgeon, once said,

> *Oh, my brothers and sisters in Christ, if sinners will be damned, at least let them leap to Hell over our bodies; and if they will perish, let them perish with our arms about their knees, imploring them to stay, and not madly to destroy themselves. If Hell must be filled, at least let it be filled in the teeth of our*

exertions, and let no one go there unwarned and unprayed for.[9]

You and I must pray for lost people and warn them of the dangers of living and dying apart from Jesus. May God help us in this dark and decadent day to be light and salt by sharing Jesus. May Christians in America experience a revival of "soul-winning." Indeed, may God help all of us as believers in Jesus for the rest of our lives to: (1) identify lost people, (2) pray for lost people, and (3) share Jesus with lost people.

And may we do it all for His glory like it matters, because it does!

---

[9] Rev. C. H. Spurgeon, "The Wailing of Risca," Vol. 7 of *Metropolitan Tabernacle Pulpit*, (Pasadena, Texas: Pilgrim Publications, 1995), 11.

Appendix A
Gospel Outline

1. Introduction
A. Family
B. Interests
C. Religious background
D. Exploratory questions

Question 1: "Do you know for certain that you have eternal life and that you will go to Heaven when you die, or would you say that is something you are still working on?"

Question 2: "If you stood before God and He asked you, 'Why should I let you into Heaven?' what would you say?"

2. Gospel Presentation
A. God loves you.

Jeremiah 31:3—"I have loved you with an everlasting love."

John 3:16—"For God so loved the world, that He gave His only begotten Son, that whoever believes in Him shall not perish, but have eternal life."

B. You are a sinner.

1 John 3:4— "Sin is lawlessness."

Romans 3:23—"For all have sinned and fall short of the glory of God."

C. God is holy and must punish sin.

Exodus 34:7—"He [The Lord] will by no means leave the guilty unpunished."

Romans 6:23—"For the wages of sin is death."

D. God sent His Son, Jesus, to save you.

- Jesus is the sinless Son of God.

  Hebrews 4:15—"[He] has been tempted in all things as we are, yet without sin."

- Jesus died for your sins and rose from the dead.

  1 Corinthians 15:3-4—"Christ died for our sins according to the Scriptures… He was buried … He was raised on the third day according to the Scriptures."

- Jesus wants to give you eternal life.

  John 3:36—"He who believes in the Son has eternal life; but he who does not obey the Son will not see life, but the wrath of God abides on him."

2 Corinthians 6:2—"Behold, now is 'the acceptable time,' behold, now is 'the day of salvation.'"

E. What must you do to be saved?

- *Repent* of your sin.

  Luke 13:3—"Unless you repent, you will all likewise perish."

  Acts 3:19—"Therefore repent and return, so that your sins may be wiped away, in order that times of refreshing may come from the presence of the Lord."

  Acts 17:30—"God is now declaring to men that all people everywhere should repent."

- *Believe* in Jesus.

  Acts 16:31—"Believe in the Lord Jesus, and you will be saved, you and your household."

  Romans 10:9—"That if you confess with your mouth Jesus as Lord, and believe in your heart that God raised Him from the dead, you shall be saved."

- *Receive* Jesus as Savior and Lord.

  John 1:12—"But as many as received Him, to them He gave the right to become children of God, even to those who believe in His name."

Romans 10:13—"Whoever will call upon the name of the LORD will be saved."

3. Commitment

A. Call for a decision.

- "If this makes sense to you, is there any *good* reason why you should not receive Jesus as your Savior and Lord right now?"
- If "Yes," review the Gospel presentation.
- If "No," proceed.

B. Clarify, and review the Gospel presentation.

- Do you understand that God loves you?
- Do you understand that you are a sinner?
- Do you understand that God is holy and must punish your sin?
- Do you understand that God sent His Son, Jesus, to save you?
- Do you understand that Jesus was sinless, yet He died for your sins and rose from the dead, and He wants to give you eternal life?
- If "Yes," proceed; if "No," review the Gospel Presentation.

C. Pray.

- "For you to understand."
- "Lead you in a prayer of surrender and commitment" (Use Gospel Presentation).
- Offer a prayer of thanksgiving.

4. Assurance

- John 6:47—"Truly, truly, I say to you, he who believes has eternal life."

- John 10:28—"And I give eternal life to them, and they will never perish; and no one will snatch them out of My hand."

5. Follow Up

- Schedule a follow-up meeting.

- Read the Bible.

- Pray.

- Fellowship.

- Share Jesus.

Appendix B
Your Personal Testimony

Use this page to write your personal testimony. Tell how you accepted Jesus as your Lord and Savior.

- Tell others what life was like before you met Jesus.

- Tell others how you came to sense your need for salvation.

- Tell others how you were converted to Christ.

- Tell others what your life is like now that you are saved.